Cofounders: Taj Forer and Michael Itkoff
Creative Director: Ursula Damm
Copy Editor: Gabrielle Fastman

ISBN: 978-1-954119-03-1

Printed by Ofset Yapimevi, Turkey

Daylight Books
E-mail: info@daylightbooks.org
Web: www.daylightbooks.org

VIEWING DISTANCE
EVAN HUME

Photography's technical and operational evolution in the twentieth century and into the twenty-first is inseparable from political conflict. Having emerged from the Second World War as the major world power, the United States wasted little time pursuing a policy of containment in the Cold War against the Soviet Union. Although the two had been allies fighting against the Axis powers, the USSR stood in the way of realizing ambitions that had driven US foreign policy since before the war—a global free enterprise system in which the US was the hegemon.[1] Containment for the US ultimately meant amplifying its global dominance through military intervention and covert operations. In 1947, the National Security Act created the National Security Council, Joint Chiefs of Staff, Central Intelligence Agency, and Department of Defense (renamed from Department of War). A rapidly growing national security state would lead to an expanded use of photography in reconnaissance and surveillance to advance the US's Cold War objectives.

The emergence of Soviet nuclear capabilities in 1949 was a cause of great alarm in the US, and the so-called bomber gap—the unfounded notion that the USSR had surpassed the US in its arsenal of bomber jets—was used to justify increased defense spending and the buildup of a bomber fleet by the US Air Force.[2] By the early 1950s, President Eisenhower and national security officials believed that innovations in aerial photo-reconnaissance were necessary to assess Soviet weapons capabilities. This new approach would be markedly different from aerial photography during the first two world wars, when cameras were used on aircraft mainly for mapping, determining potential bombing targets, and assessing damage after raids. "Peacetime" aerial photography's goal became capturing images of Warsaw Pact military installations while avoiding detection by Soviet radar systems. The results of this photographic desire were significant developments in aerial imaging as well as high-altitude and high-speed aircraft created from a partnership between government agencies, corporations, and academia now commonly referred to as the military-industrial complex.

The US had already been conducting aerial reconnaissance over the USSR using Boeing RB-47 aircraft equipped with cameras and radar tracking devices since the late 1940s. Moscow made it known such reconnaissance flights had been tracked, but it did not initially react militarily.[3] In 1950, the USSR enacted a more assertive air defense policy and attacked all aircraft coming near its borders. If the US wanted to continue attempting to gather intelligence about Soviet aircraft and weapons capabilities, it would have to completely rethink its approach. Two early proponents of producing new high-altitude aircraft for photo-reconnaissance were Richard Leghorn, a former Kodak employee, and Edwin Land, inventor of instant film and founder of Polaroid. Both men had connections to the military-industrial complex and became directly involved in the development

---

1 Perry Anderson, *American Foreign Policy and Its Thinkers* (New York: Verso, 2015), 17.
2 Ibid., 64.
3 Gregory Pedlow and Donald Welzenbach, *The Central Intelligence Agency and Overhead Reconnaissance: The U-2 and Oxcart Programs 1954–1974* (Washington, DC: Center for the Study of Intelligence), 3.

of projects dedicated to reconnaissance aircraft. Leghorn had led Army reconnaissance groups during the Second World War and became a lieutenant colonel in charge of the Reconnaissance Systems Branch at Wright Air Development Command. He was transferred to the Pentagon in 1952, where he met other like-minded engineers interested in high-altitude reconnaissance photography and advocated for the development of a new aircraft. Branches of the US Air Force began exploring design possibilities for new aircraft with the Lockheed Corporation joining the competition in 1953. In 1954, Lockheed's Clarence "Kelly" Johnson submitted a glider-inspired design called the CL-282, which was estimated to have a maximum altitude of just above 70,000 feet. Land served on government scientific advisory boards and eventually secured permission from the Eisenhower administration to move forward on the project and commissioned Harvard scientist James Baker to develop a high-resolution camera system and Kodak to create special film. Because of the lightweight structure required for the aircraft to be effective at the desired elevation, the plane had no guns—its main function was to operate as a high-flying camera. Top Air Force officials were unhappy with the aircraft's lack of weapon systems and soon lost interest in the project.[4] President Eisenhower and his advisors agreed that the CIA should take charge of the operation, despite the resistance of Director of Intelligence Allen Dulles, who preferred more traditional methods of espionage. Eisenhower gave the CIA no choice, considering this to be primarily an intelligence-gathering operation and not a military one. He believed a mission operated by a civilian agency carried less risk of causing political damage if a reconnaissance aircraft was detected or crashed within the borders of the USSR.

Renamed the U-2 under Project Aquatone, the spy plane's high operational altitude required a complex camera system. Scientists were at first skeptical that useful photographs could be captured from even 40,000 feet. An effective model had to be at least four times as powerful as aerial cameras at the time. Baker designed lenses using an algorithm on an IBM Card-Programmed Calculator that modeled the effects of various design attributes. This is an origin point of cybernetic photography. The camera systems that Baker developed were capable of capturing photographs with a resolution 240 percent greater than any existing camera. The CIA's once-skeptical Allen Dulles was impressed by images from a 1956 flight over Soviet bases, which he would later call "million-dollar" photography.[5]

Knowing that Soviet radar systems would inevitably improve, the CIA's Scientific Engineering Institute (SEI) explored ways of reducing targeting and tracking of the U-2. SEI determined that this could be achieved by flying at supersonic speeds and efforts turned to developing a reconnaissance aircraft that was both high-altitude and high-speed. Edwin Land would again play a leading role in development. The CIA's chosen design of the Lockheed A-12, also designed by Kelly Johnson, became the foundation of Project Oxcart. The new aircraft would fly at a supersonic speed of Mach

---

4 Pedlow and Welzenbach, 12.
5 Ibid., 111.

3.2 (2,455 mph or 3,951 km/h), five times faster than the U-2, and reach an altitude of 90,000 feet. Project Oxcart enlisted Hycon, Kodak, and Perkins-Elmer to each create camera systems "that would provide a range of photography from high-ground-resolution stereo to extremely high-resolution spotting data."[6] Project Oxcart's A-12 and the SR-71 variant were the most advanced aircraft that had ever been built and were ready for operational use by 1965. However, new computer-operated radar systems in the USSR made Oxcart's supersonic speed no longer a guaranteed defense against detection. Instead of conducting flights over Soviet bases, Oxcart aircraft were used in a limited capacity for photo-reconnaissance over Vietnam under Operation Black Shield. Project Oxcart was ended by mid-1968 due to concerns over funding and sustainability.[7]

The successful CORONA satellite program that was being developed in parallel with Project Aquatone and Project Oxcart would become the lodestar for clandestine photo-reconnaissance moving forward. In 1968, President Johnson stated, "We've spent 35 or 40 billion on the space program. And if nothing else had come out of it except the knowledge that we gained from space photography, it would be worth ten times what the whole program had cost."[8] While this invaluable photography ultimately proved that the bomber gap was a myth and that the Soviet arsenal was not nearly as large as once assumed, intelligence gathering by satellites and eventually drones would be an essential part of the national security state's preservation and expansion of US global dominance.

The source images that make up the pictures in *Viewing Distance* provide a distorted and fragmented archival glimpse of photography in the service of US imperium. While many of the images date back to the mid-twentieth century, they have only recently been declassified and much information remains secret. These pictures represent the decades-long time delay from when knowledge comes into being and when it becomes publicly accessible. Some are deliberately concealed while others have transformed by repeated reproduction during their time in the archives. *Viewing Distance* combines photographs pertaining to Cold War developments in photographic technologies with contemporary documents and devices, connecting past and present with implications for the future. Processes including analog printing, digital collage, scanner manipulation, and data bending are used to animate the archival material. Through this disruption and layering, historical fragments are presented in a state of flux, open to alternate associations and implications. What we are allowed to know and see is often incomplete and indeterminate, encouraging speculation and critical vision.

—Evan Hume

6 Ibid., 281.
7 Ibid., 304.
8 Evert Clark, "Satellite Spying Cited by Johnson," *The New York Times*, March 17, 1968.

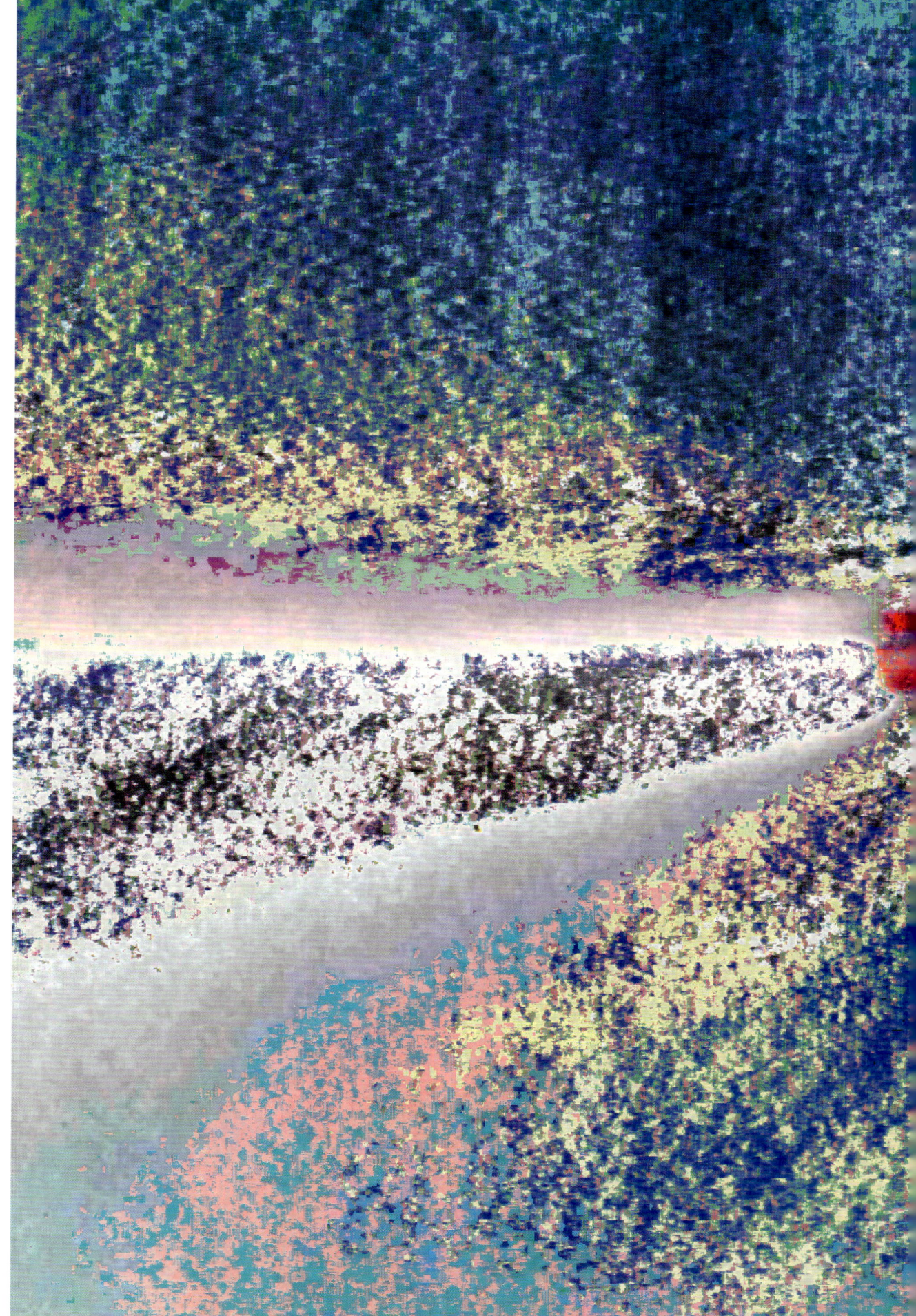

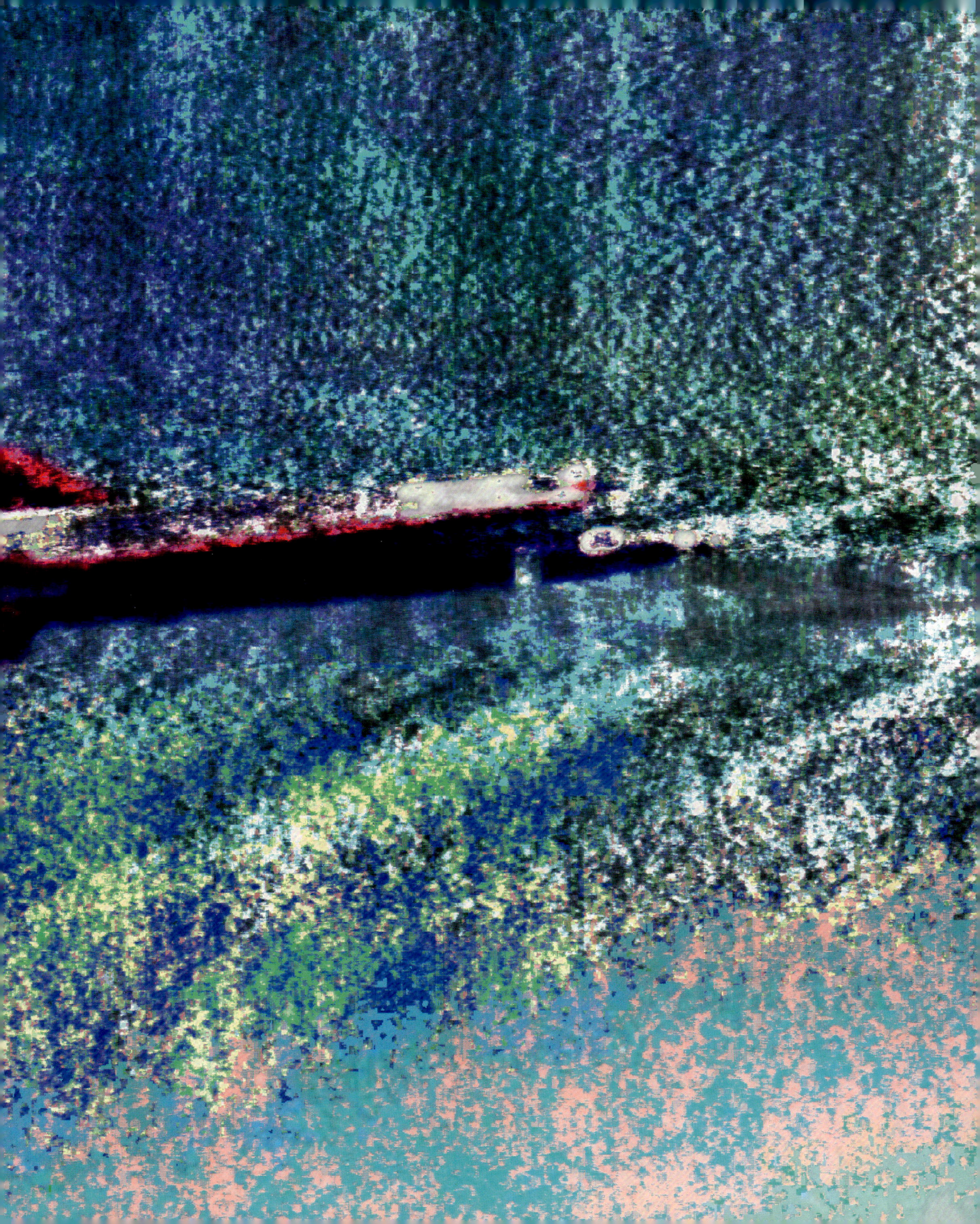

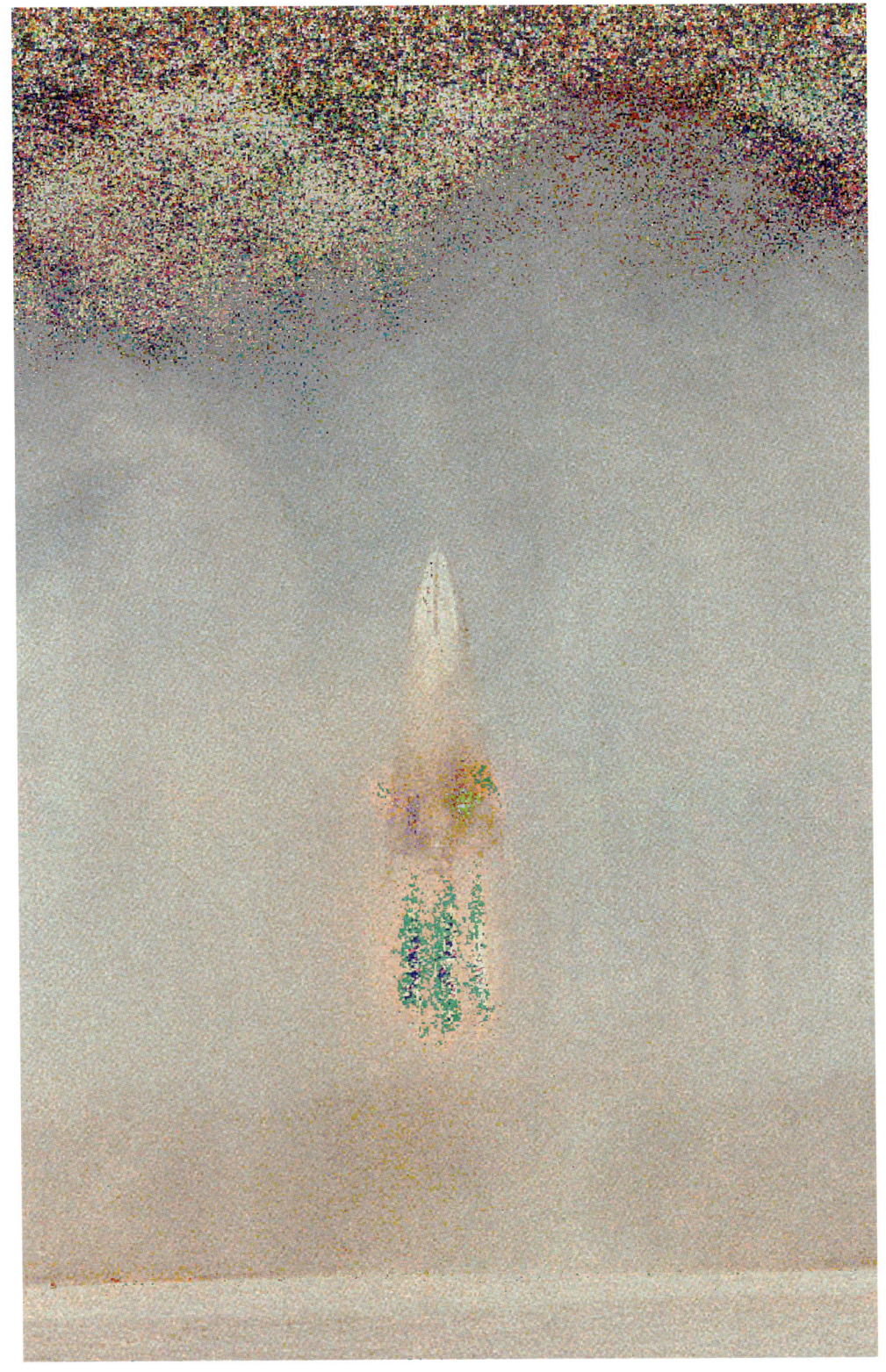

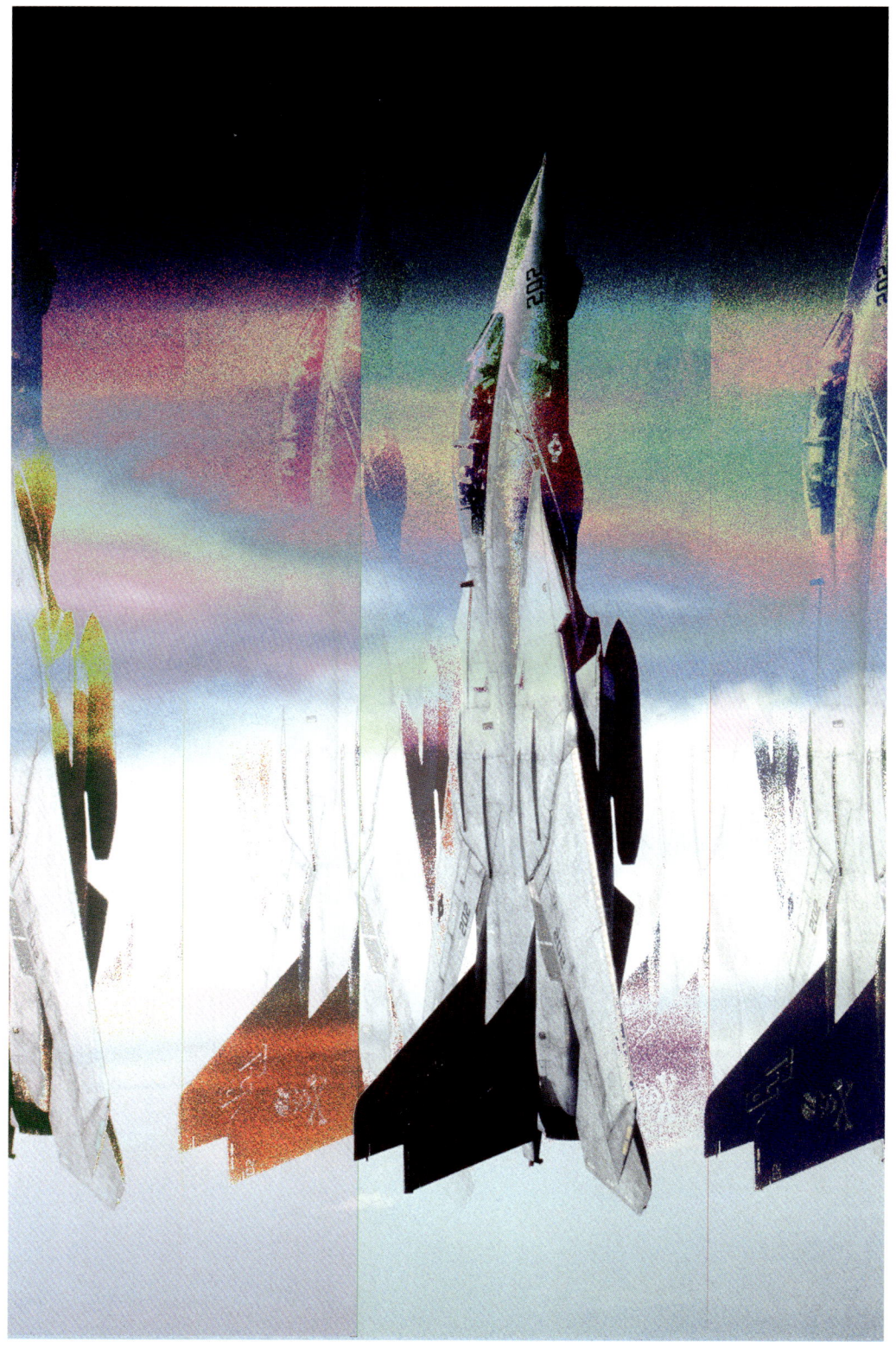

VD_12

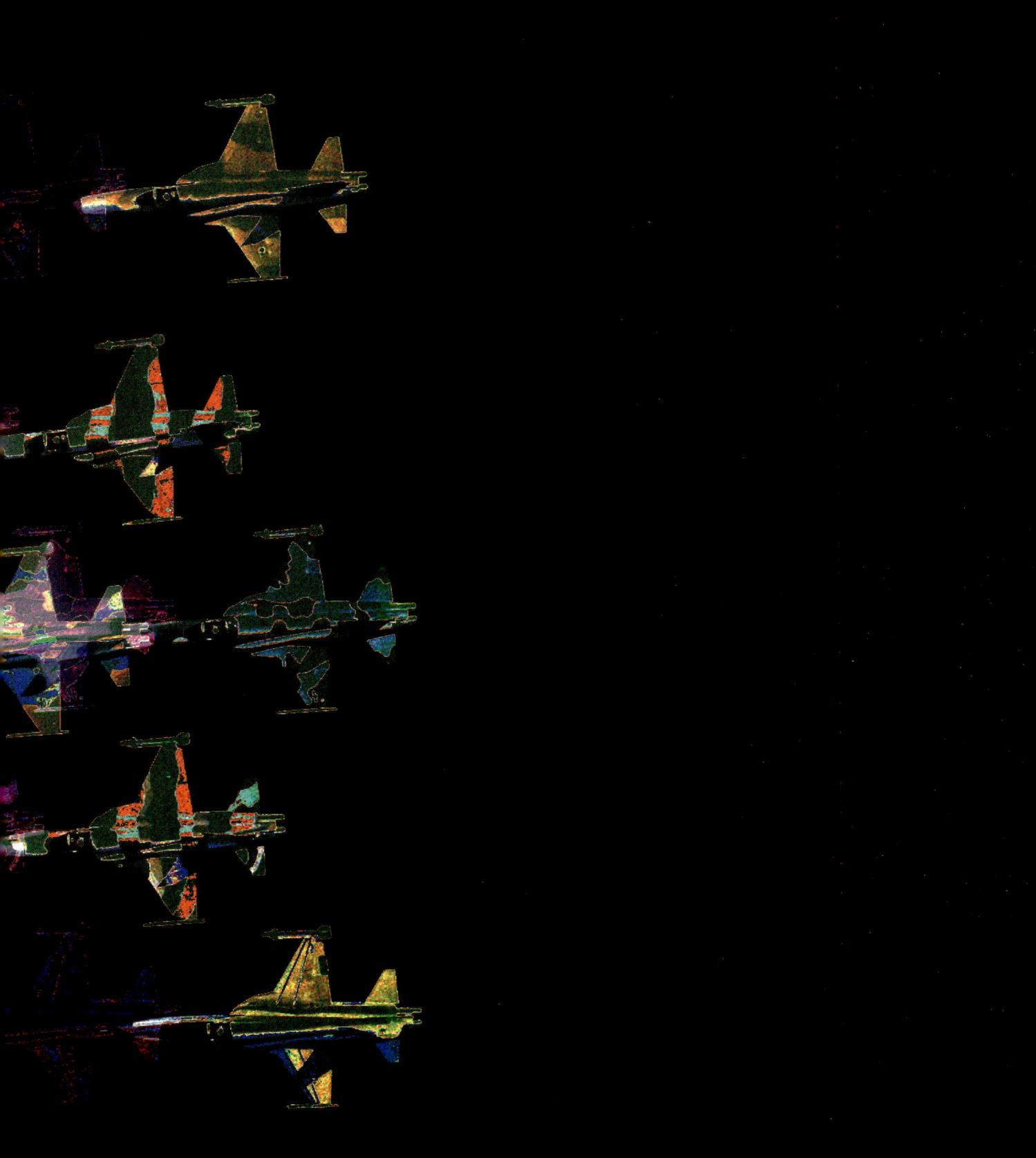

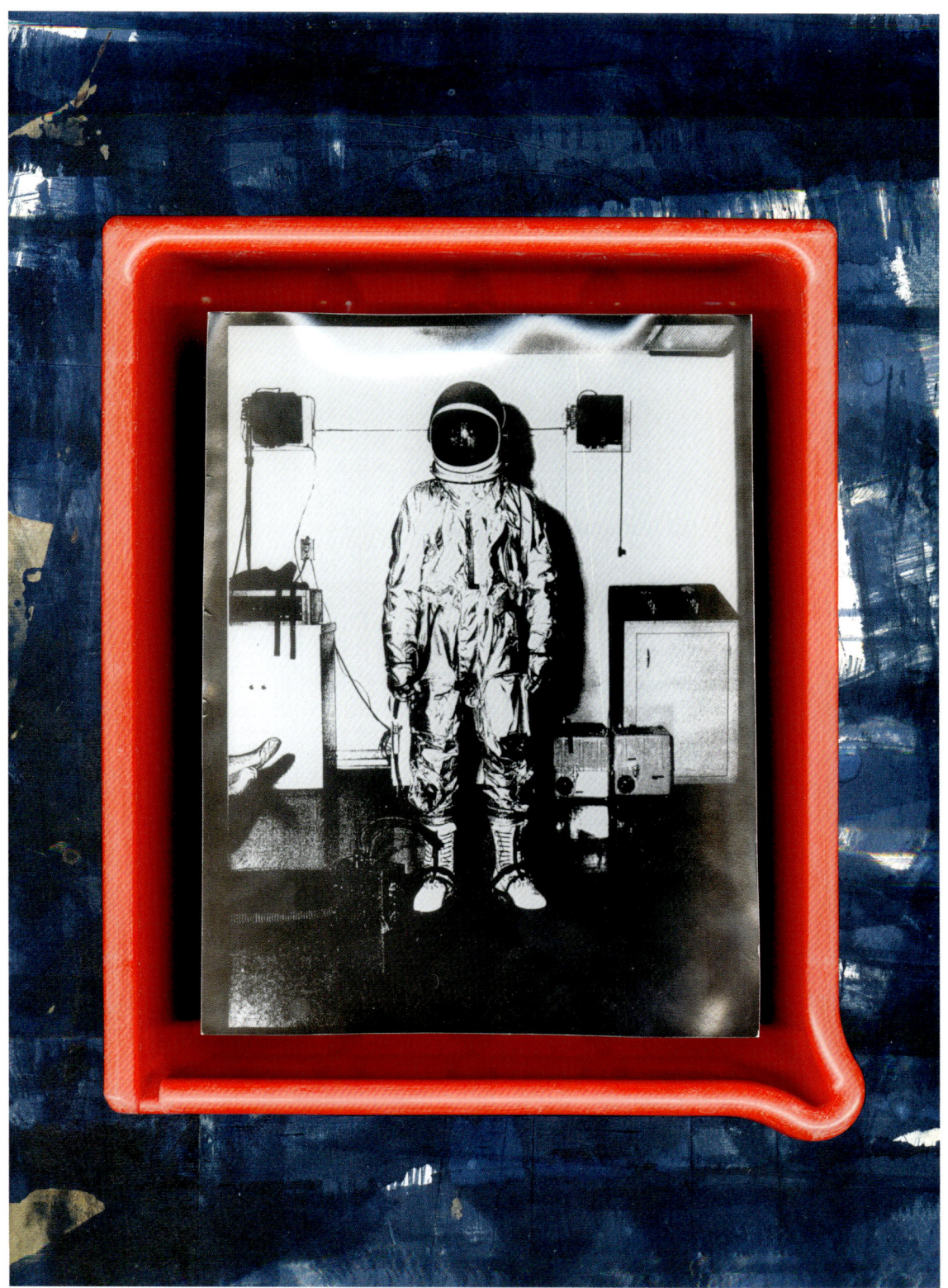

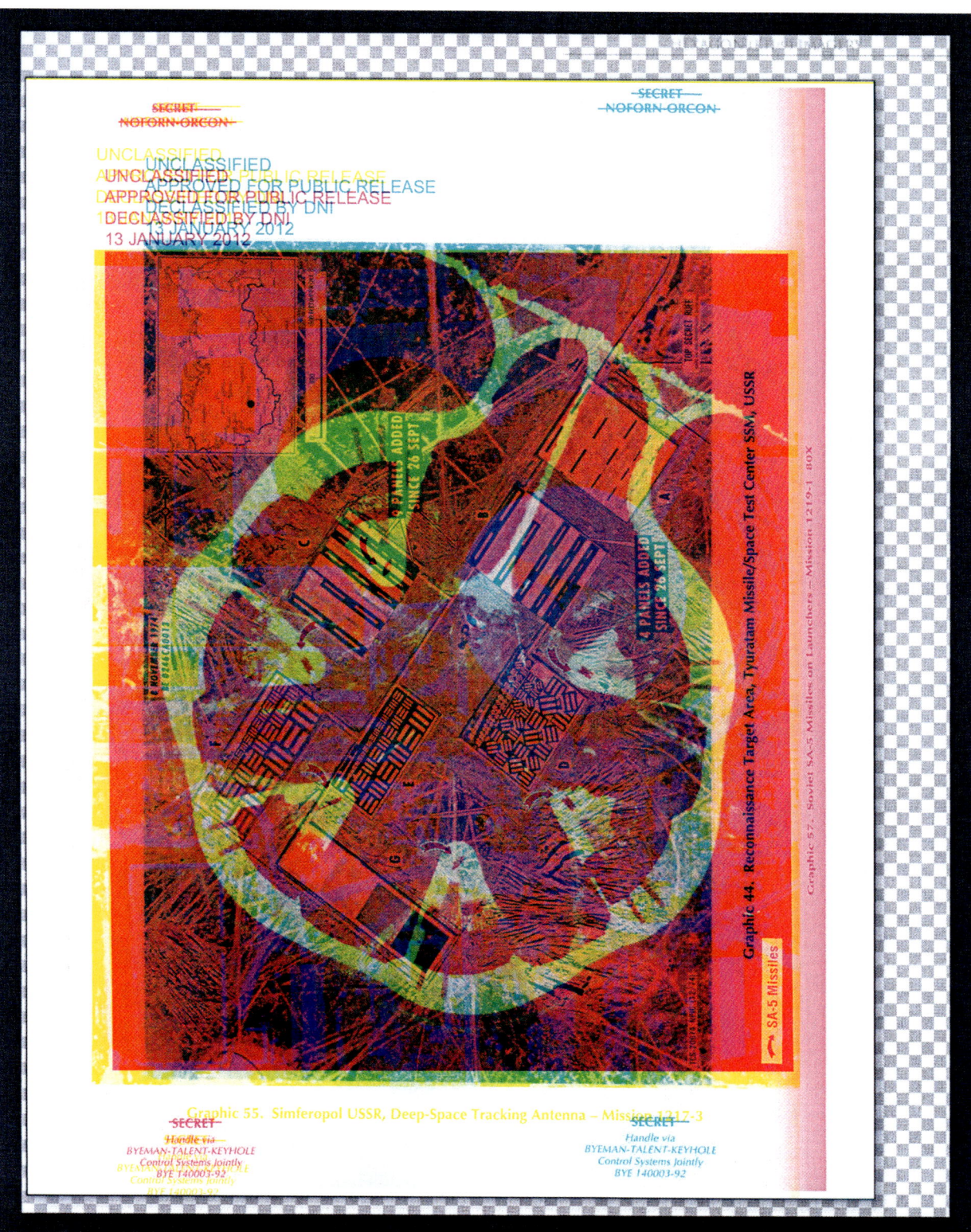

Graphic 44. Reconnaissance Target Area, Tyuratam Missile/Space Test Center SSM, USSR

Graphic 57. Soviet SA-5 Missiles on Launchers – Mission 1219-1 80X

PANELS ADDED SINCE 26 SEPT

PANELS ADDED SINCE 26 SEPT

SA-5 Missiles

Graphic 55. Simferopol USSR, Deep-Space Tracking Antenna – Mission 1217-3

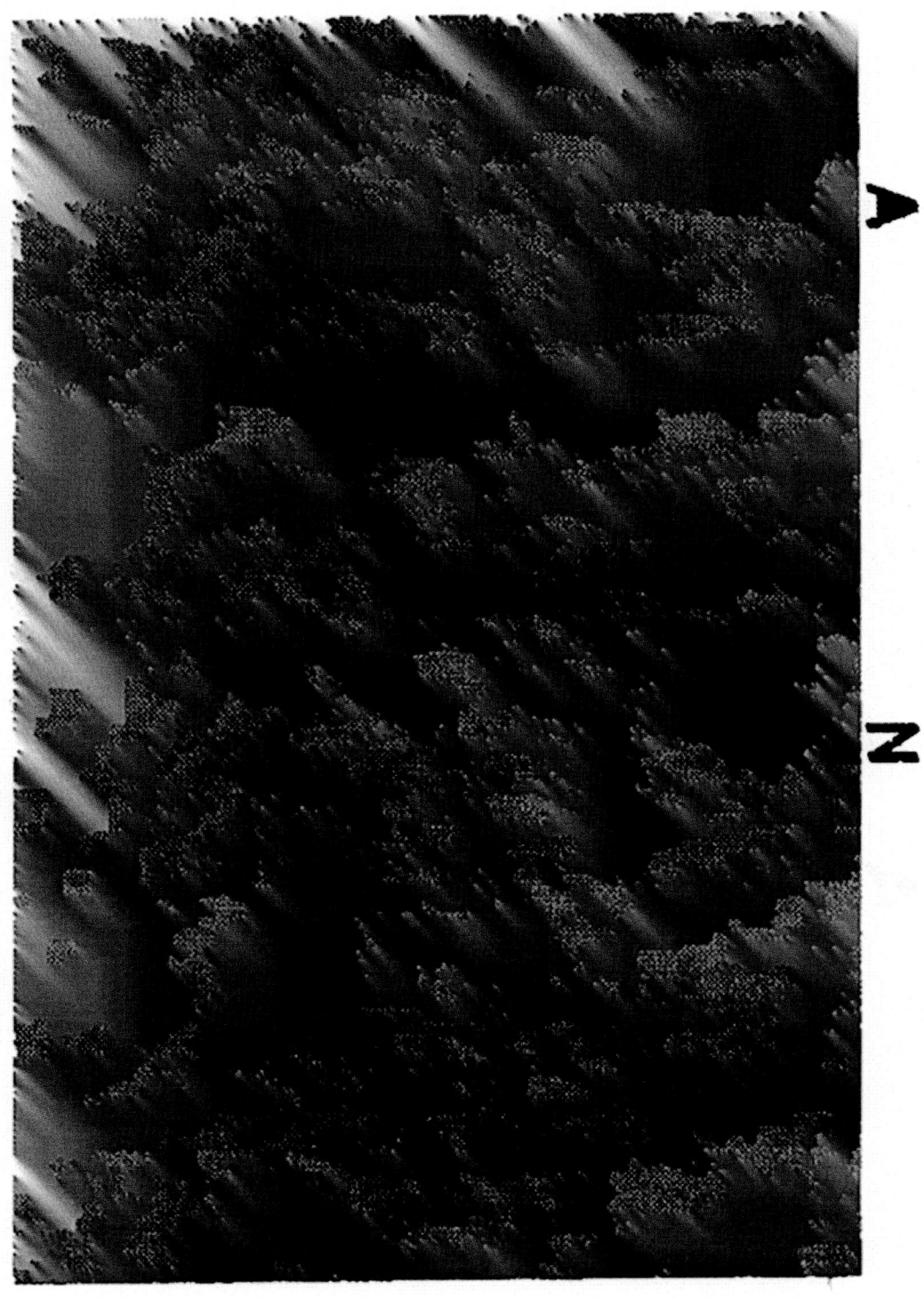

VD_ 21

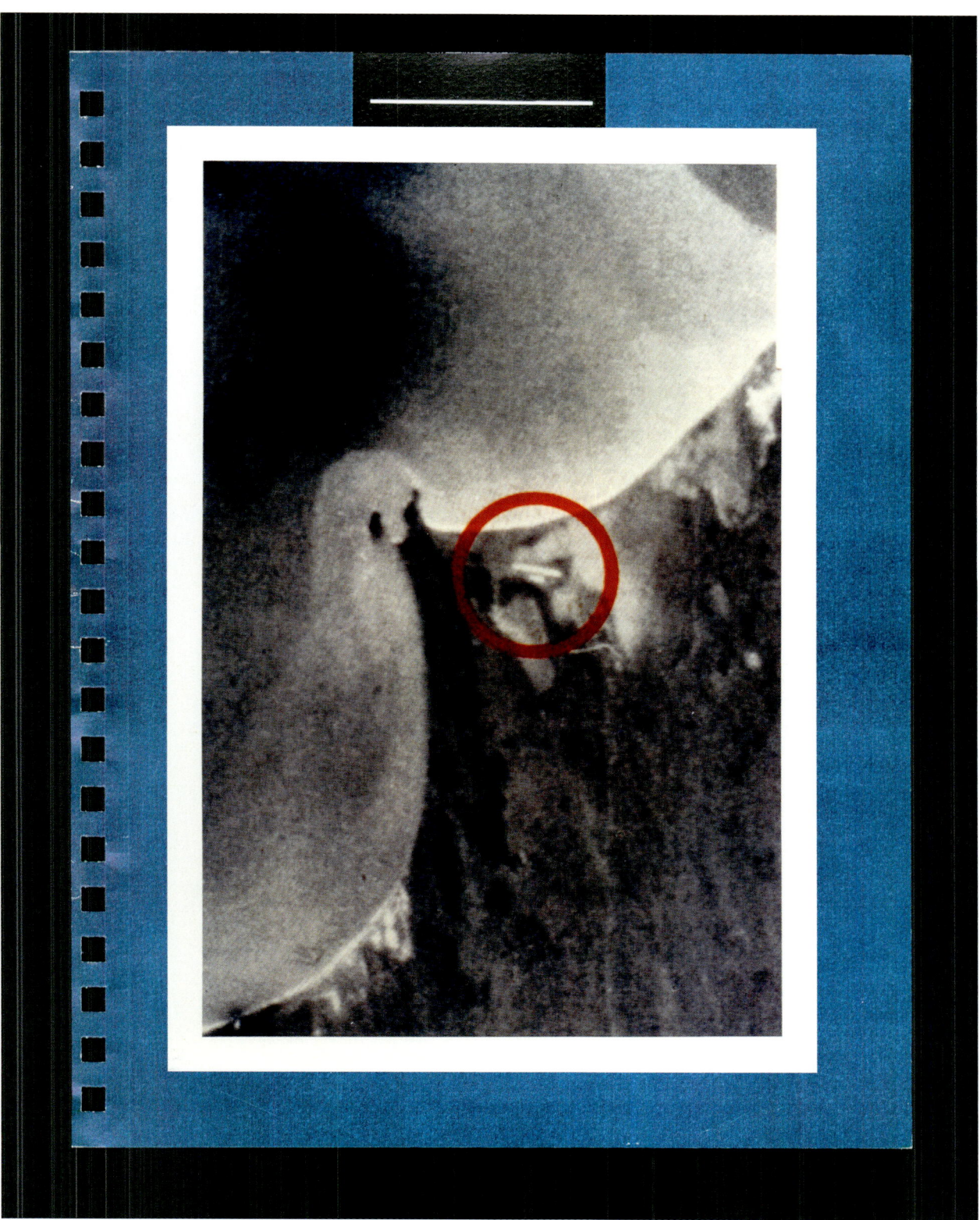

VD_23

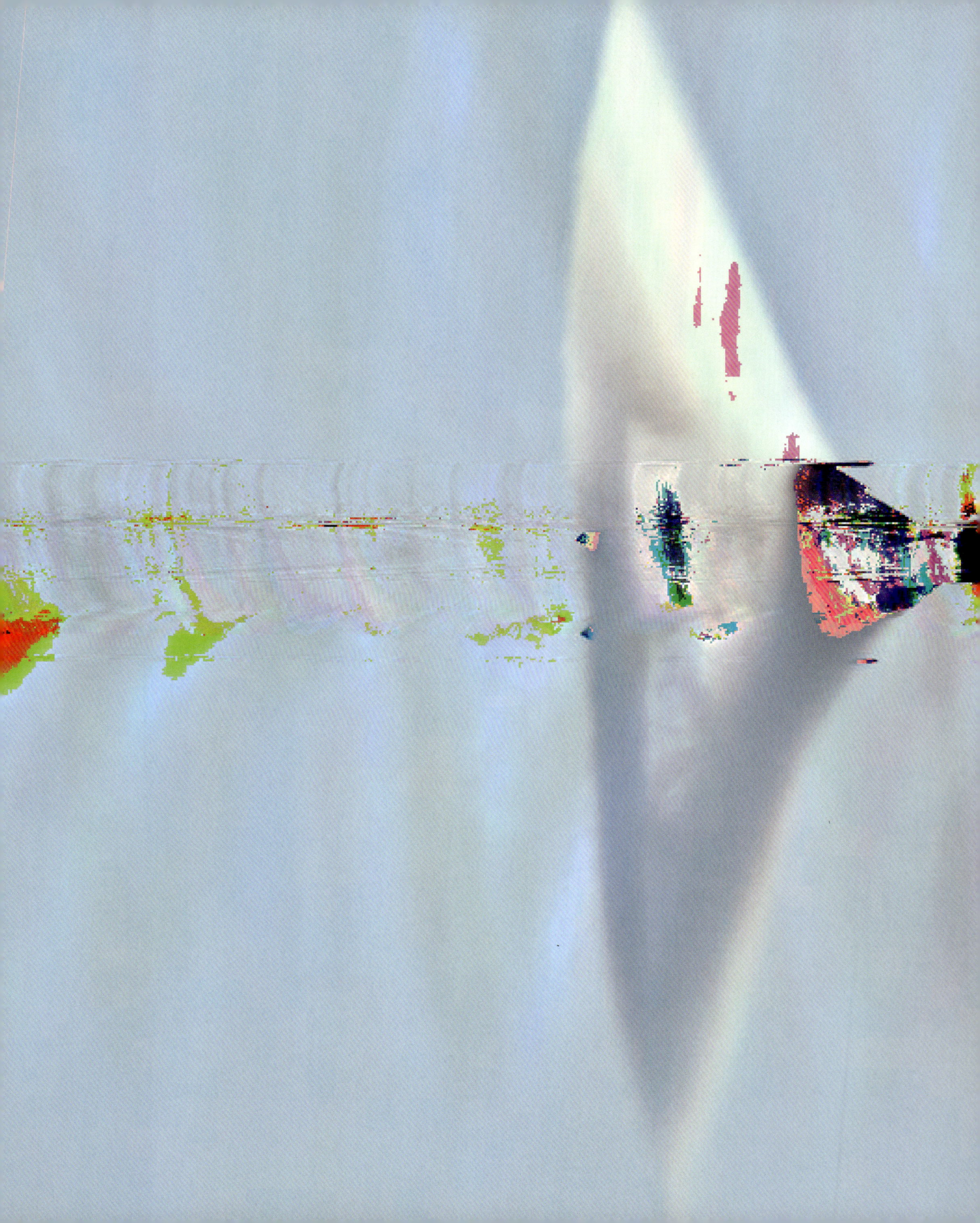

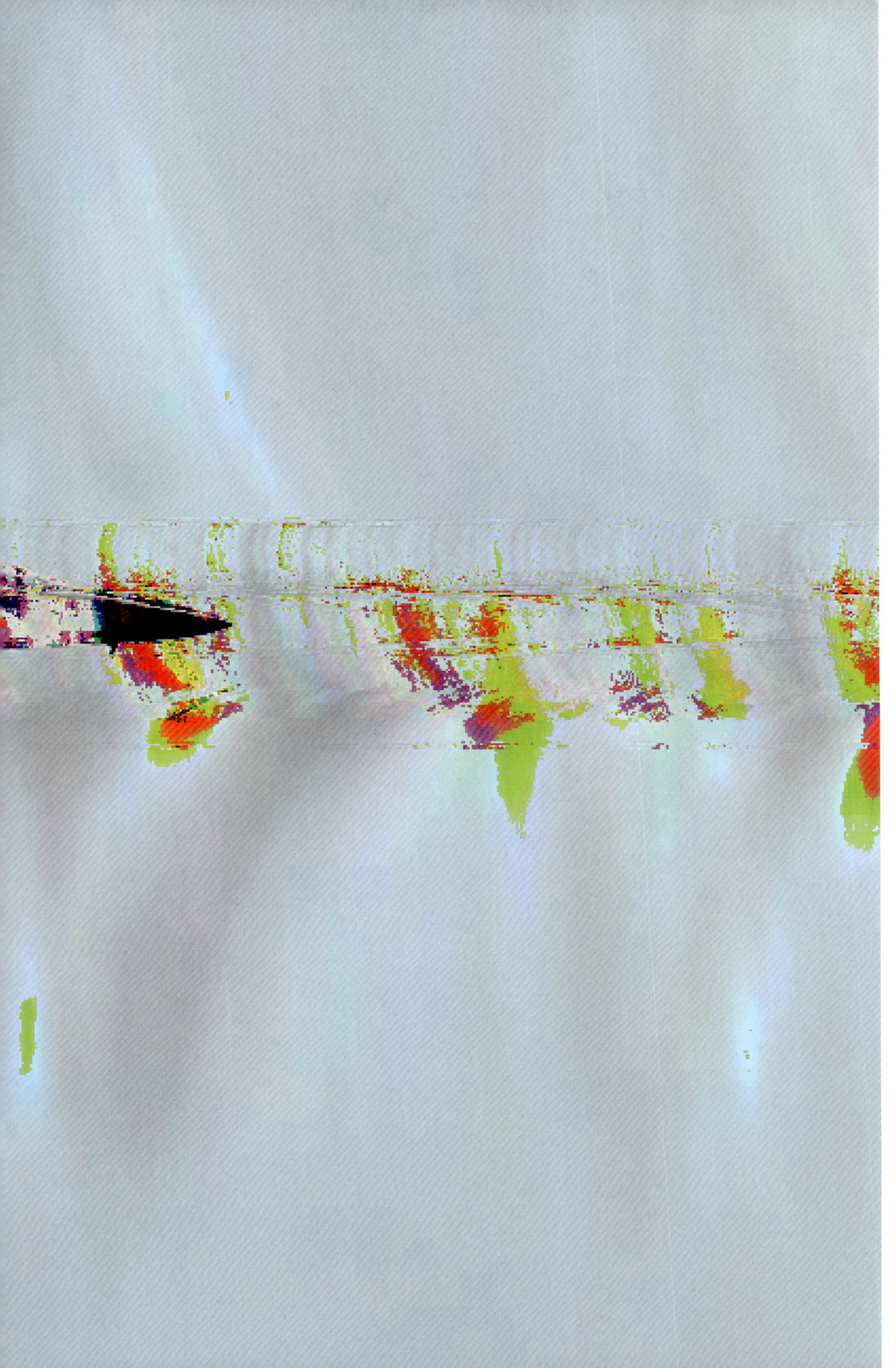

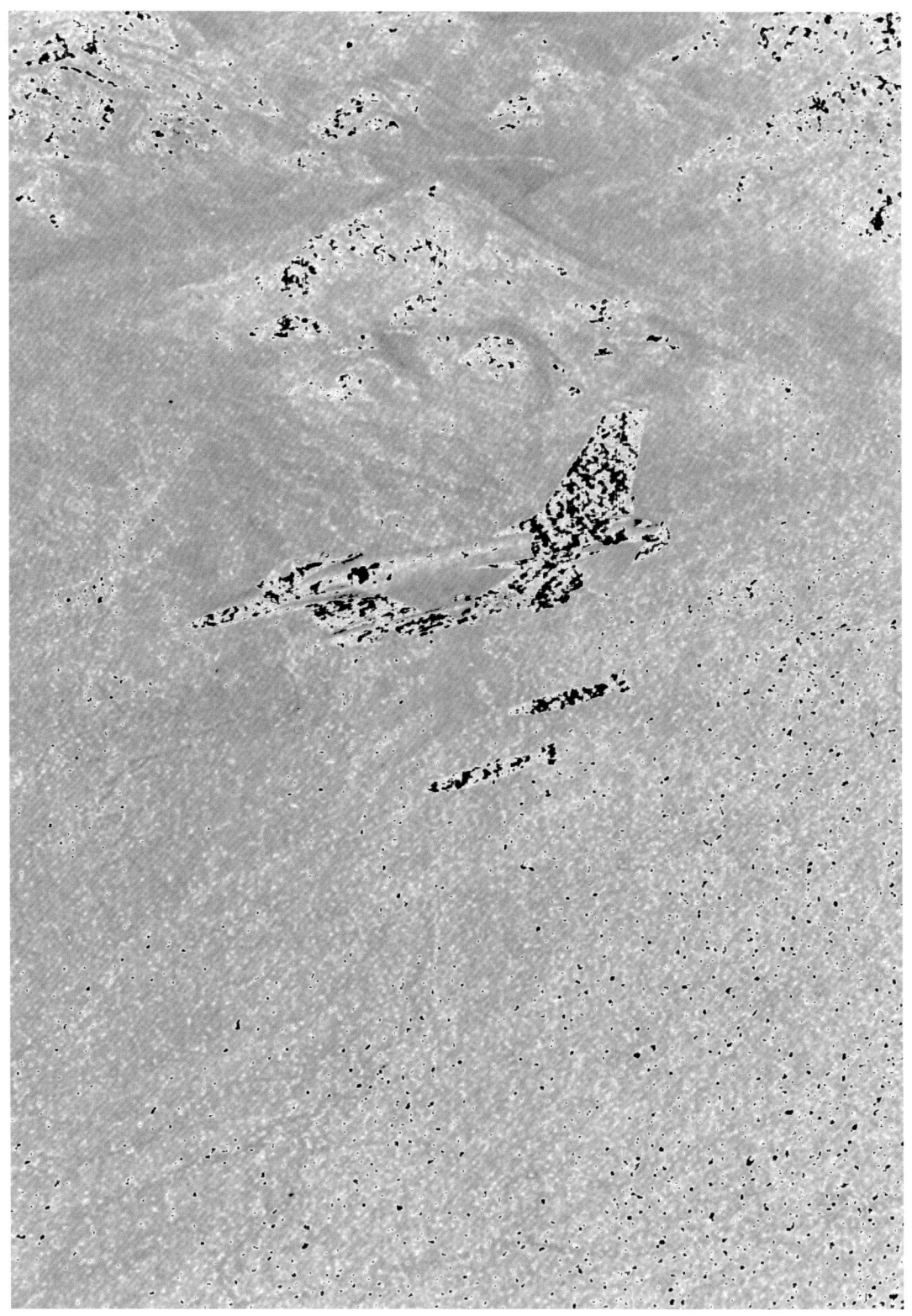

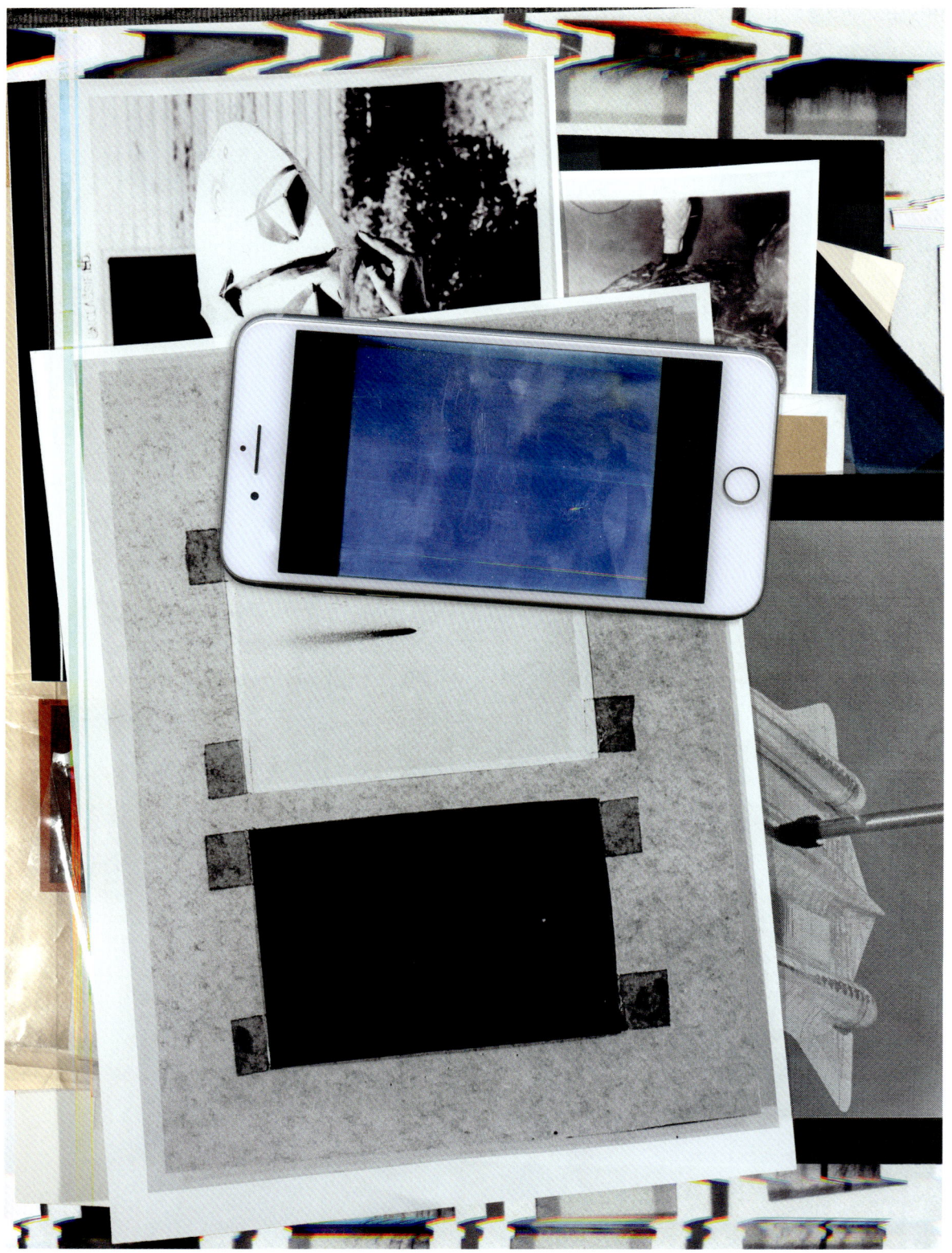

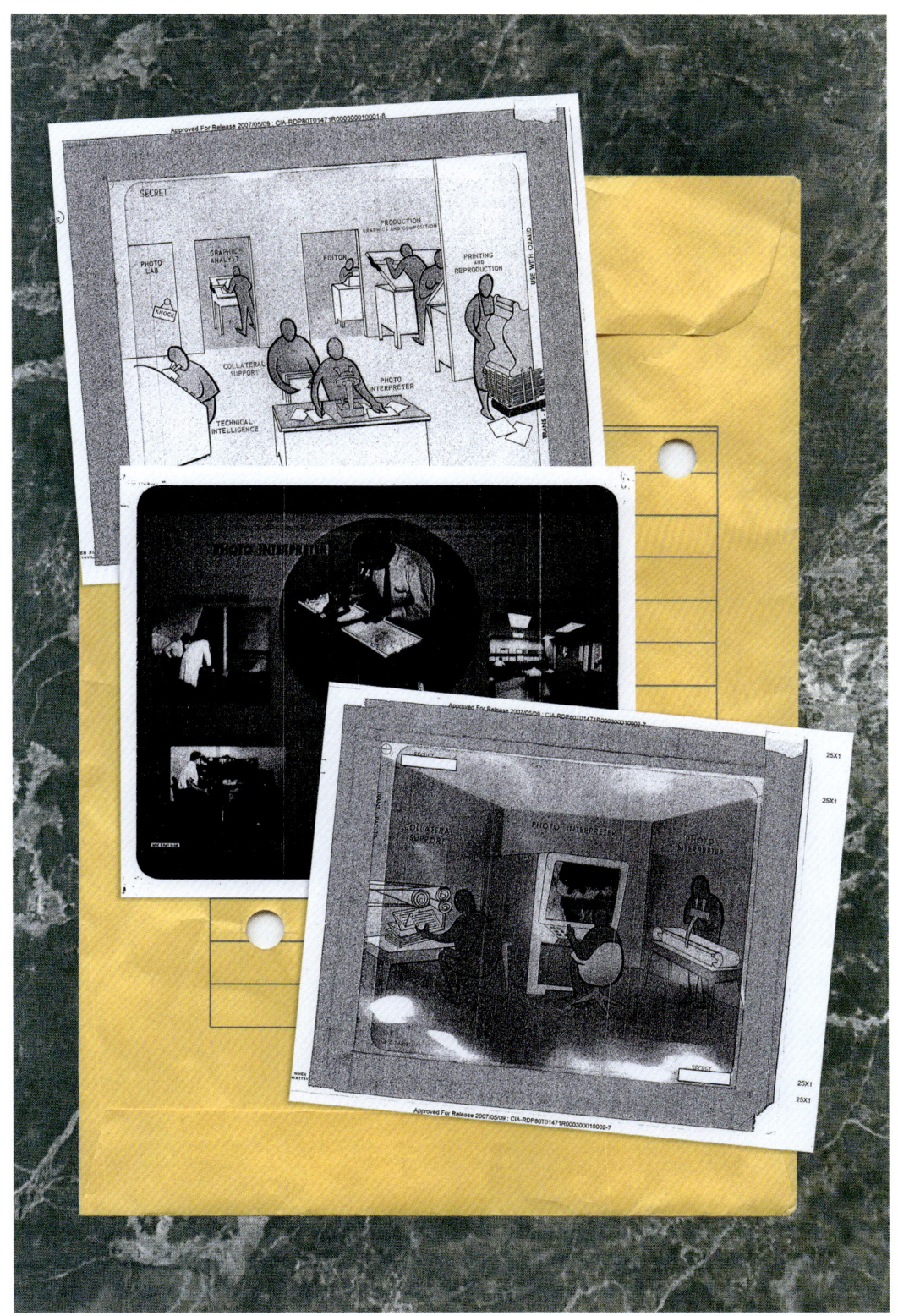

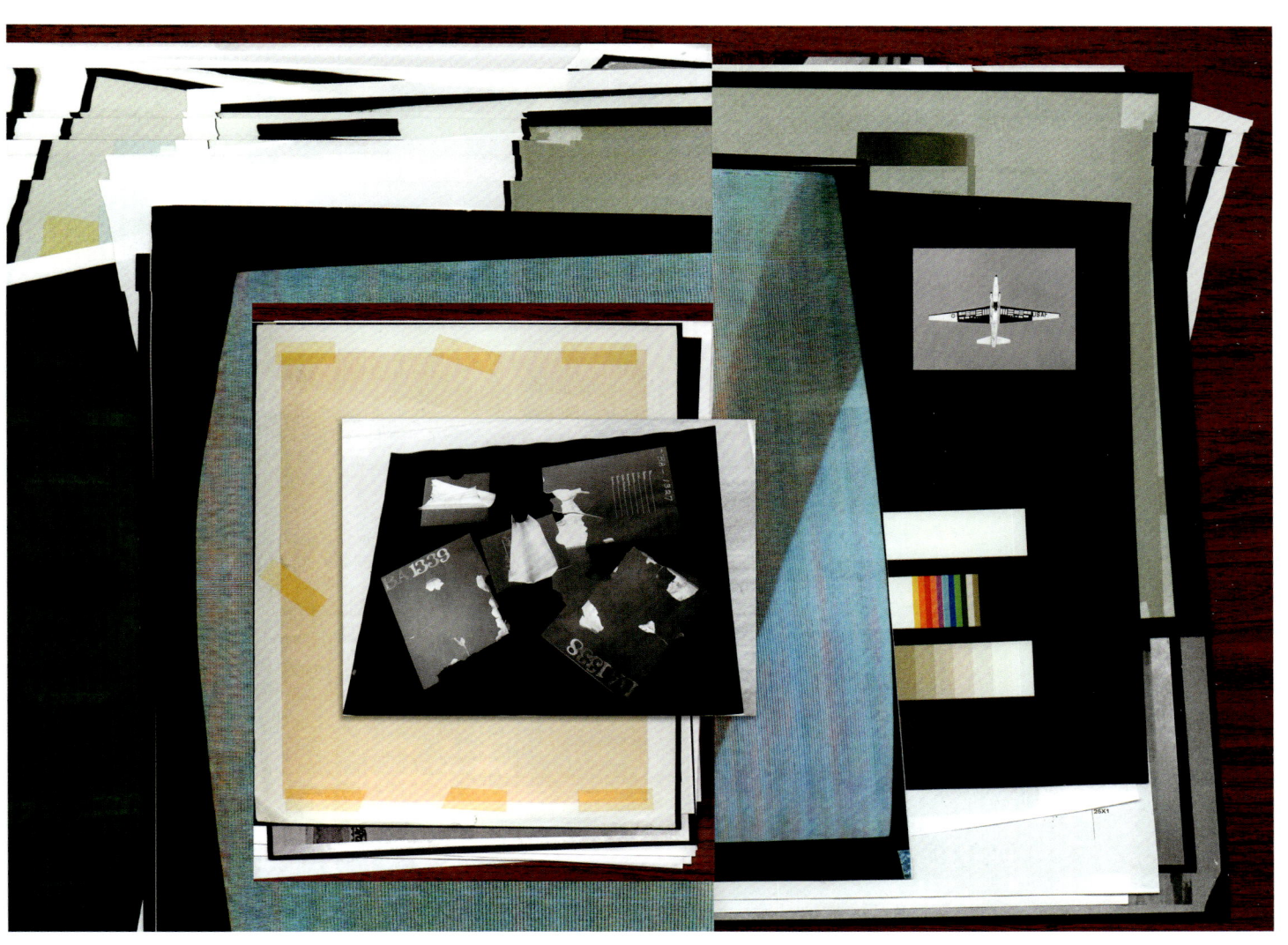

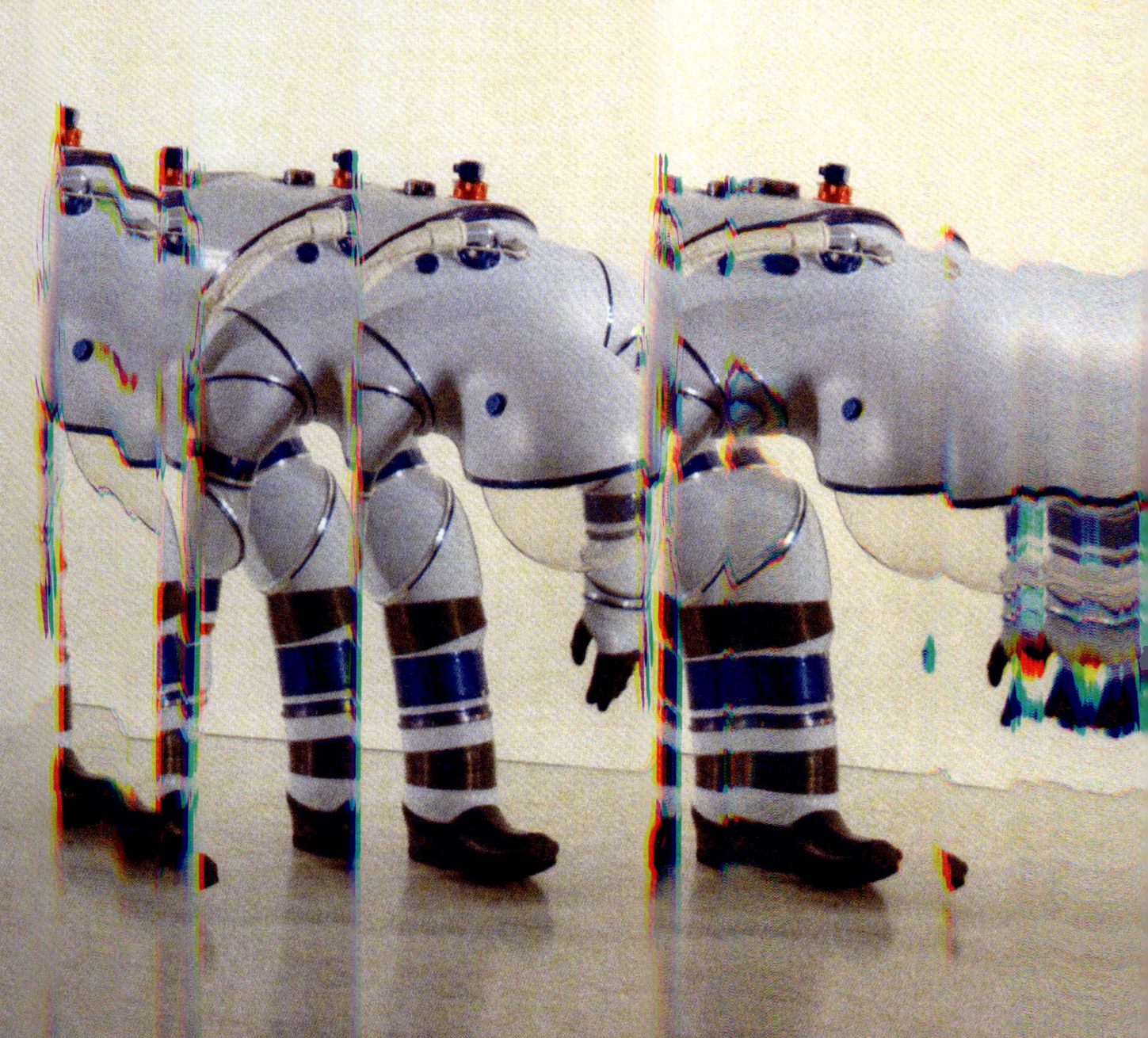

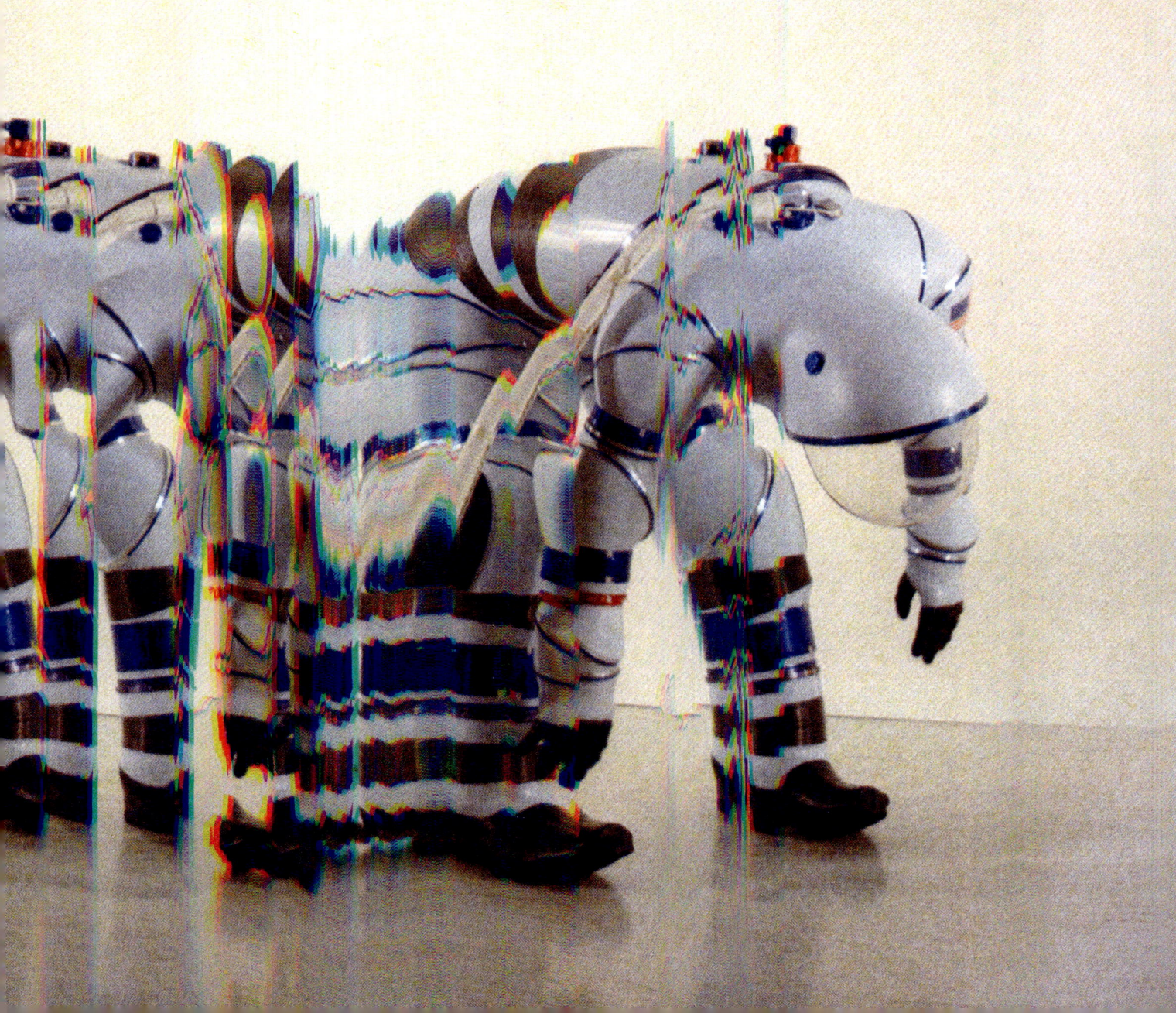

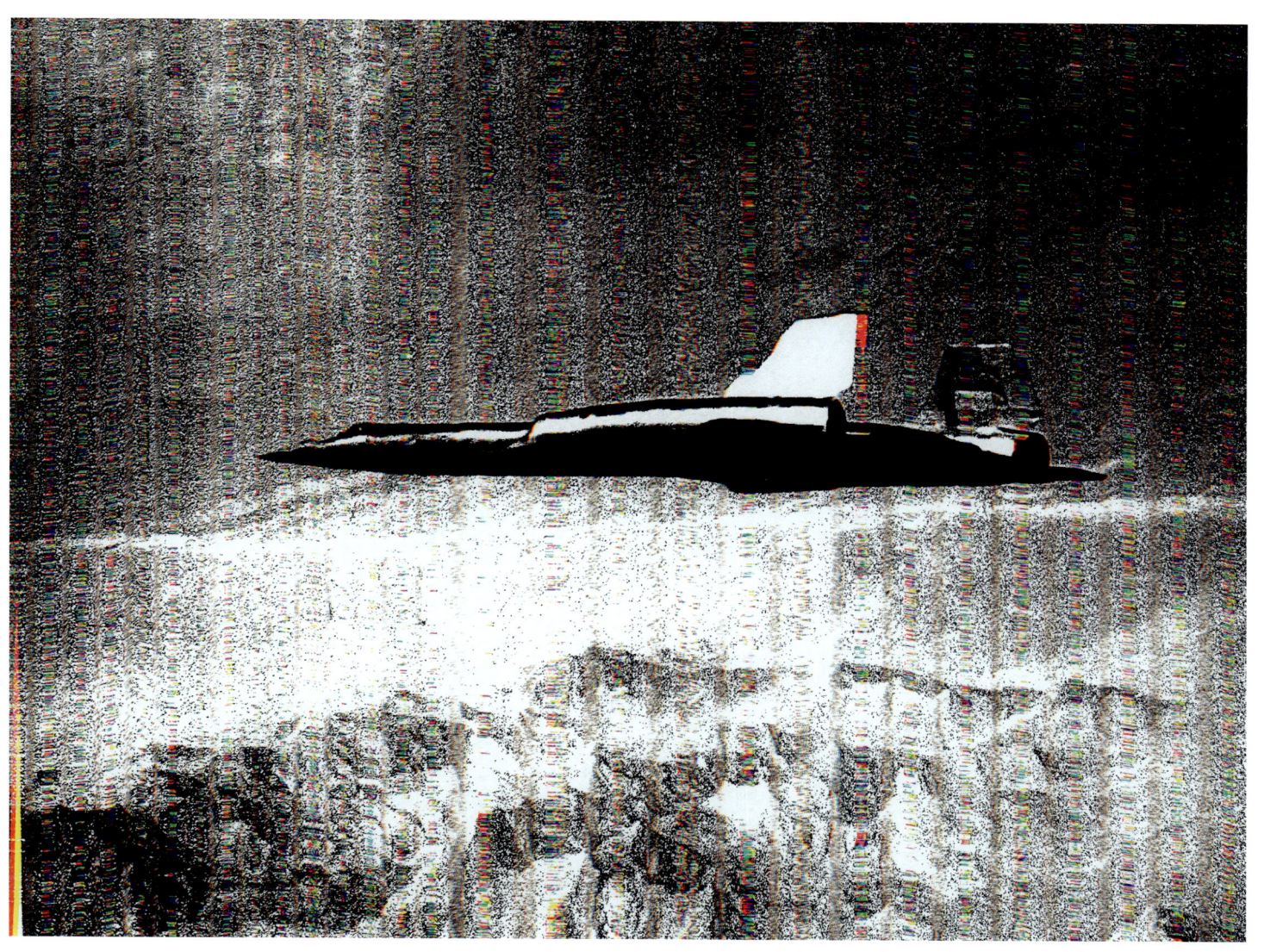

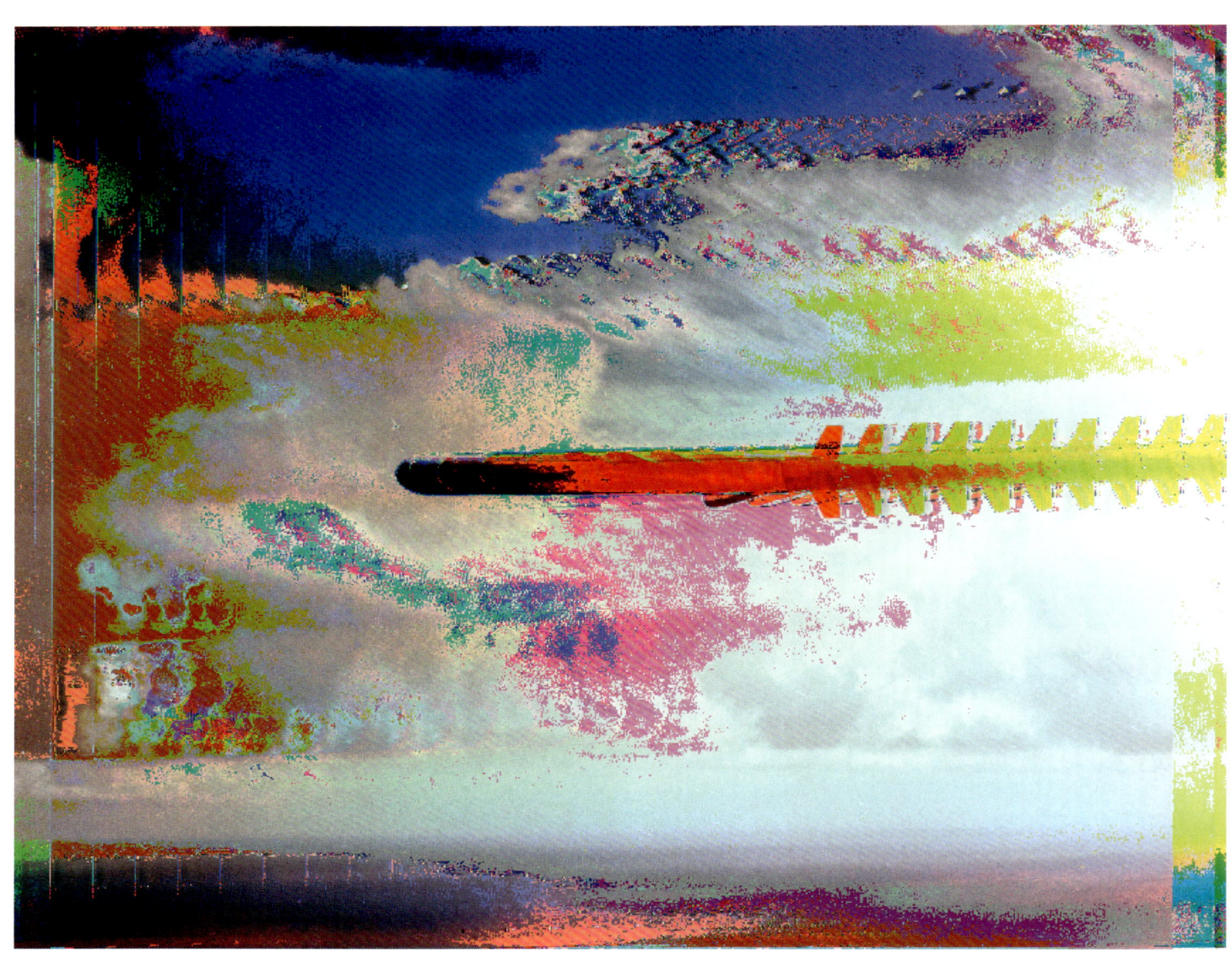

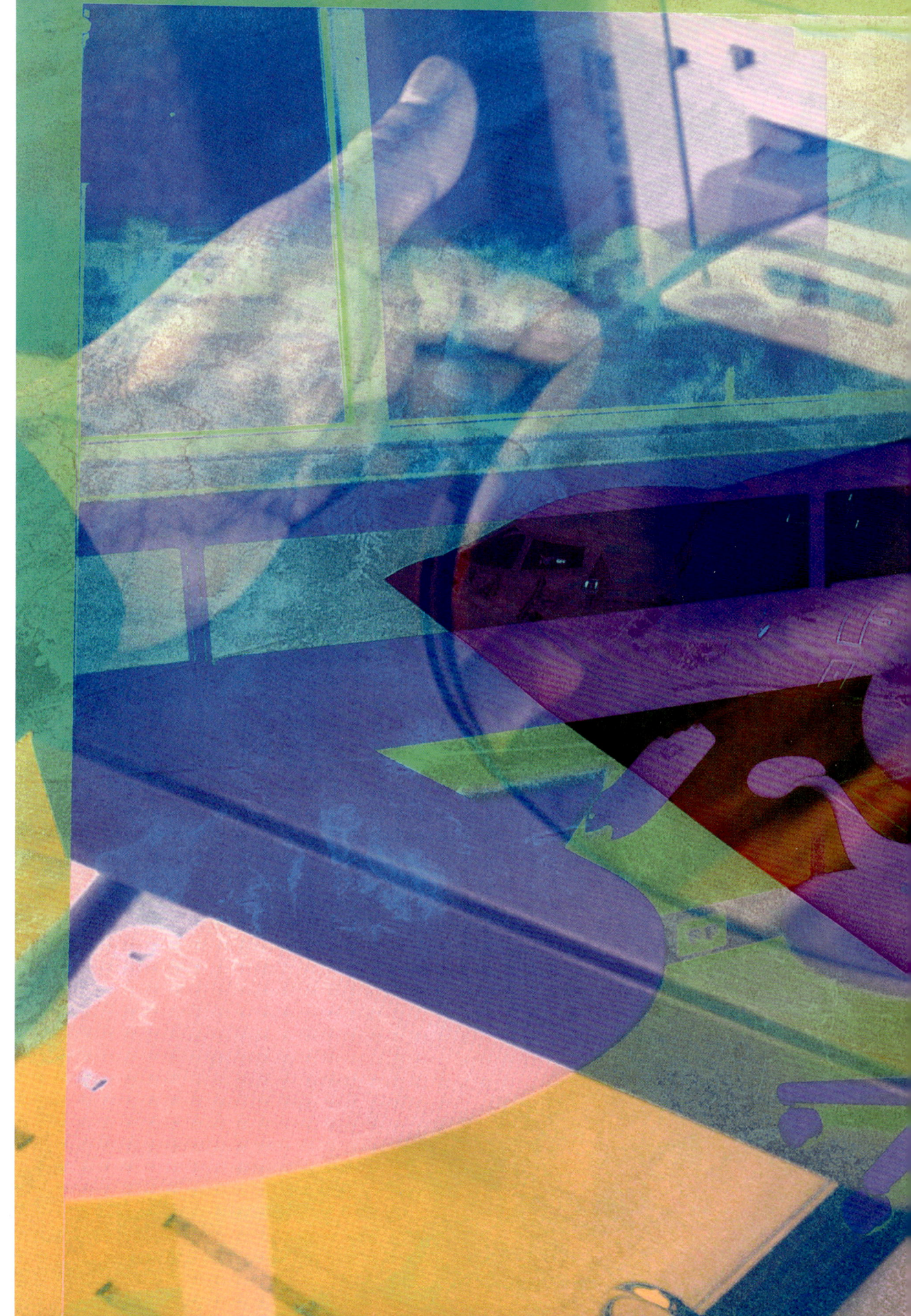

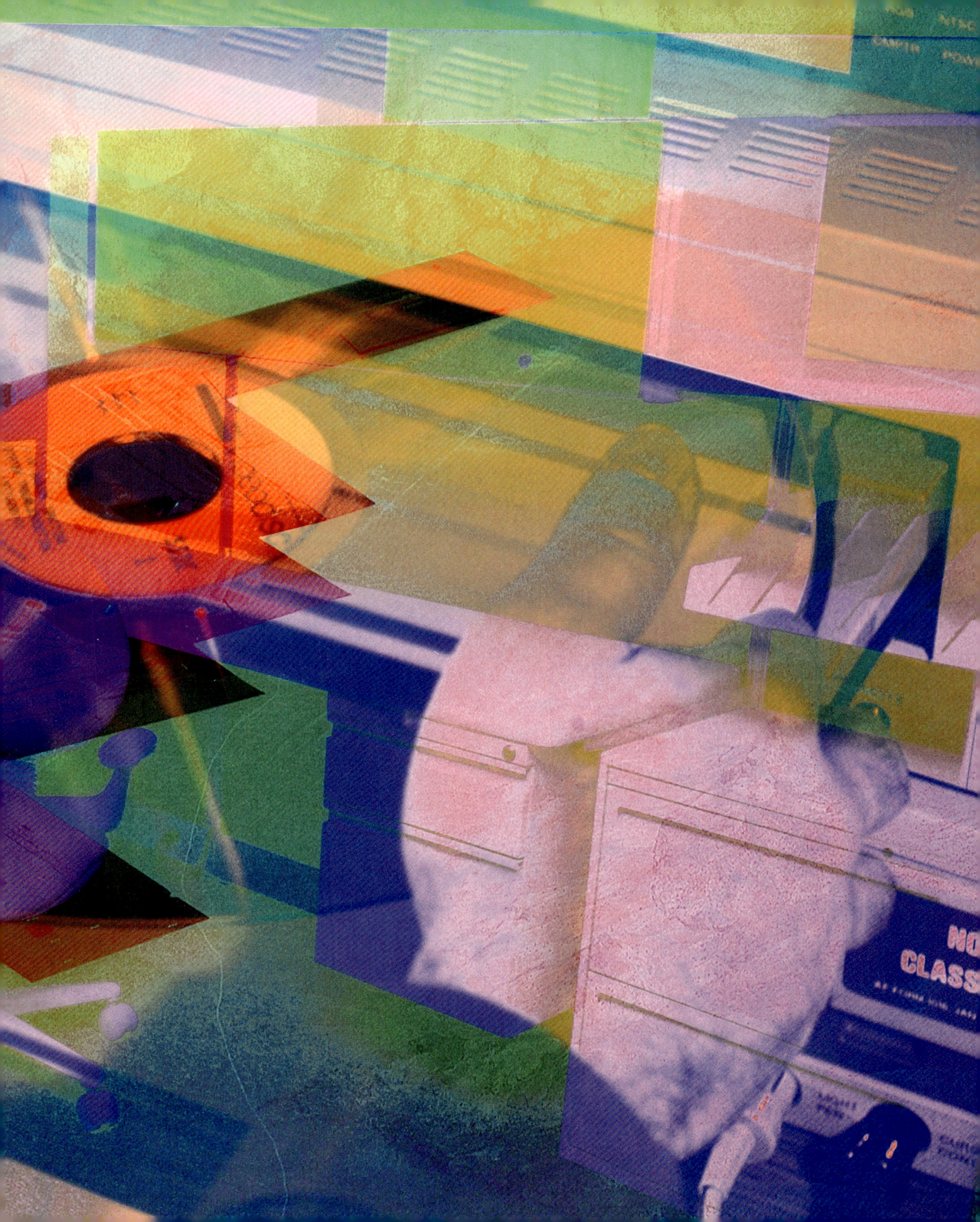

Fighting in the war against terrorism

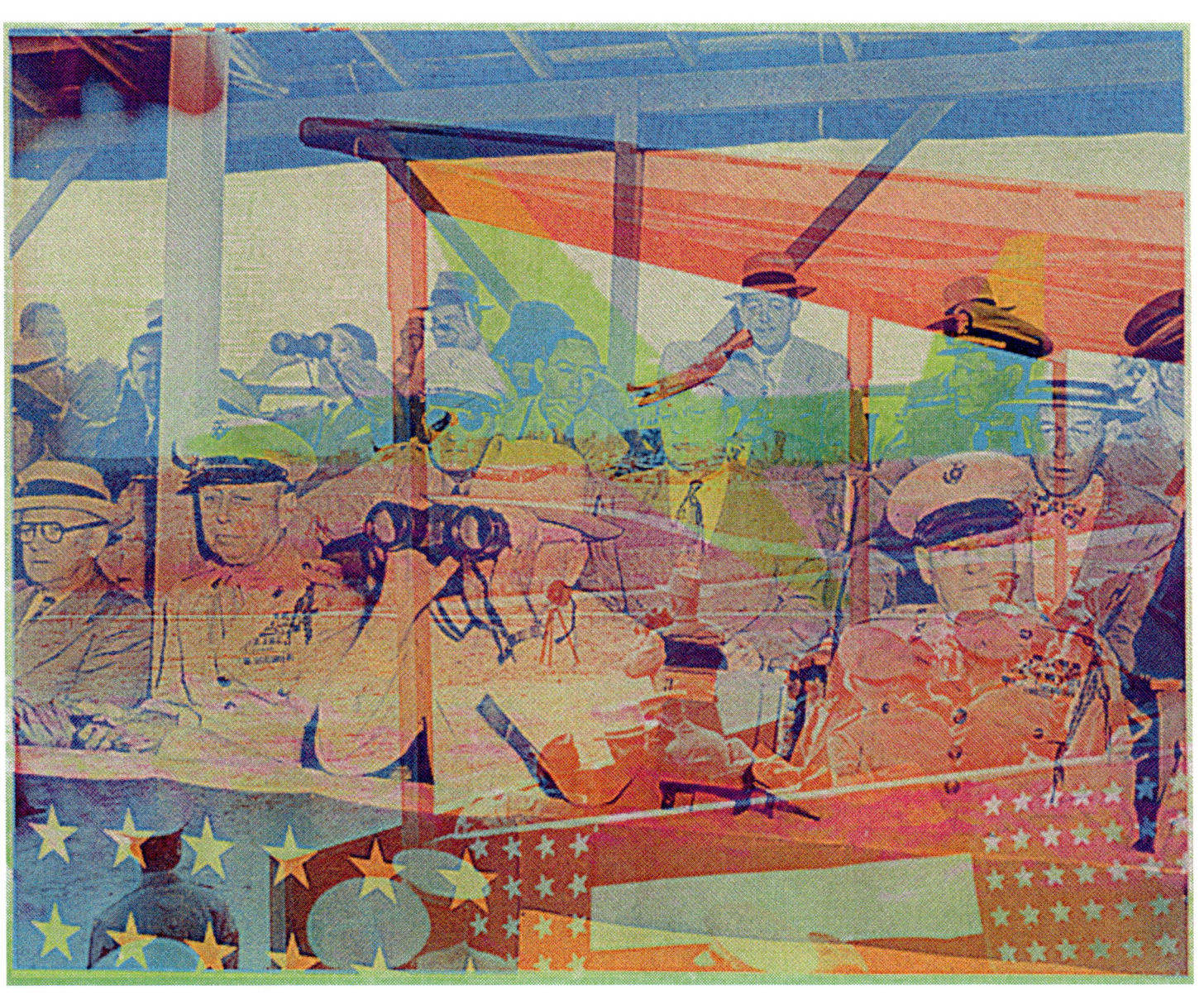

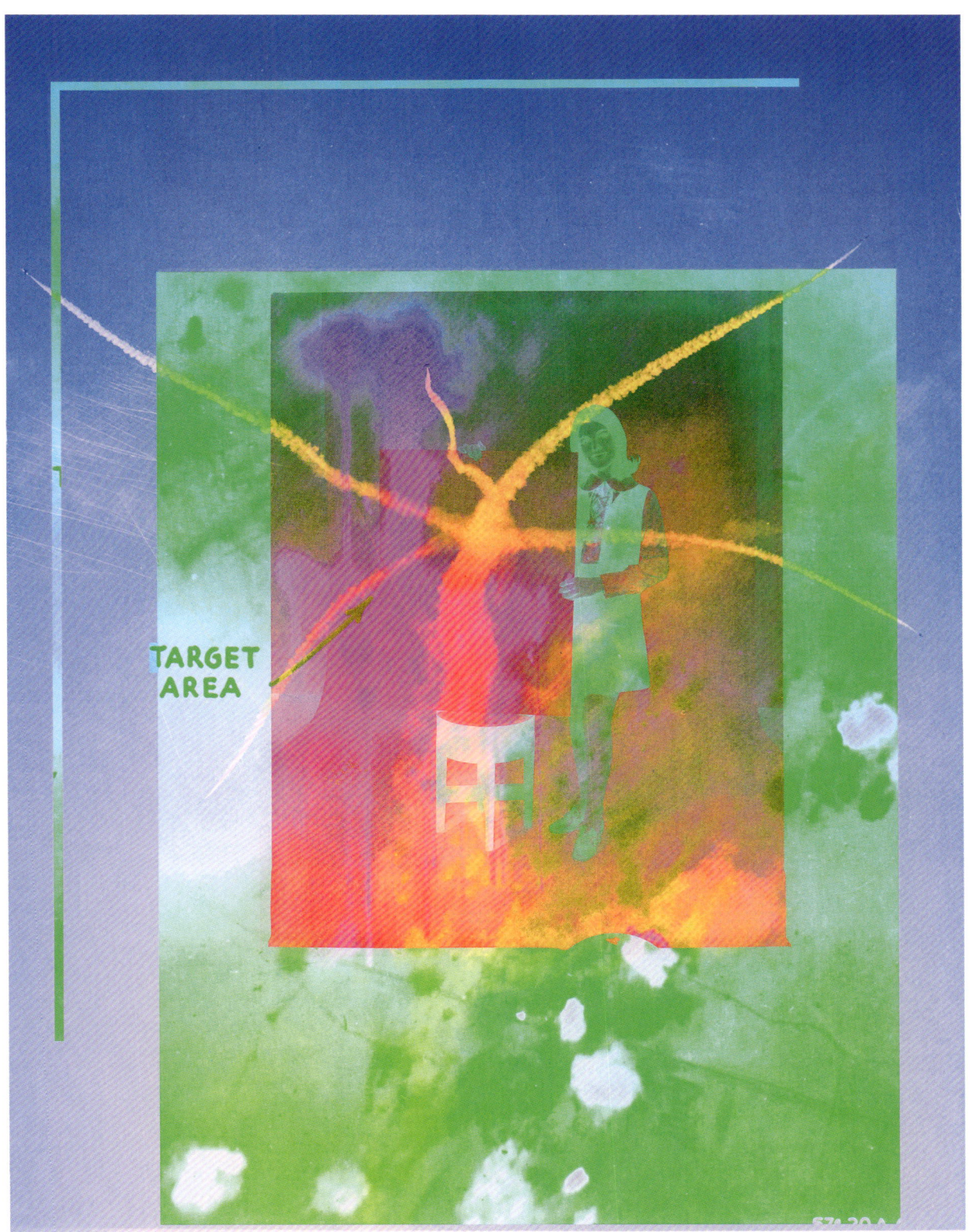

TARGET
AREA

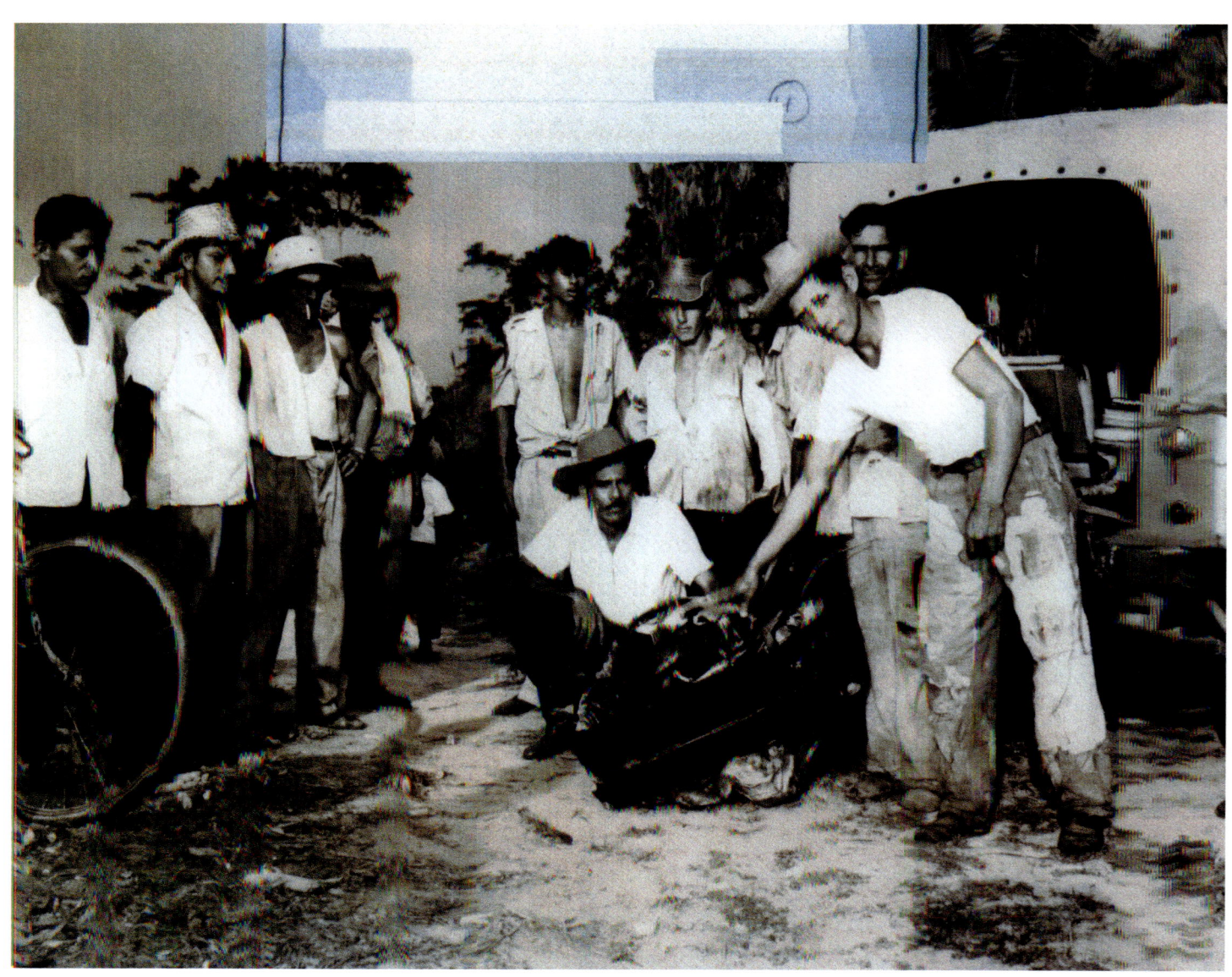

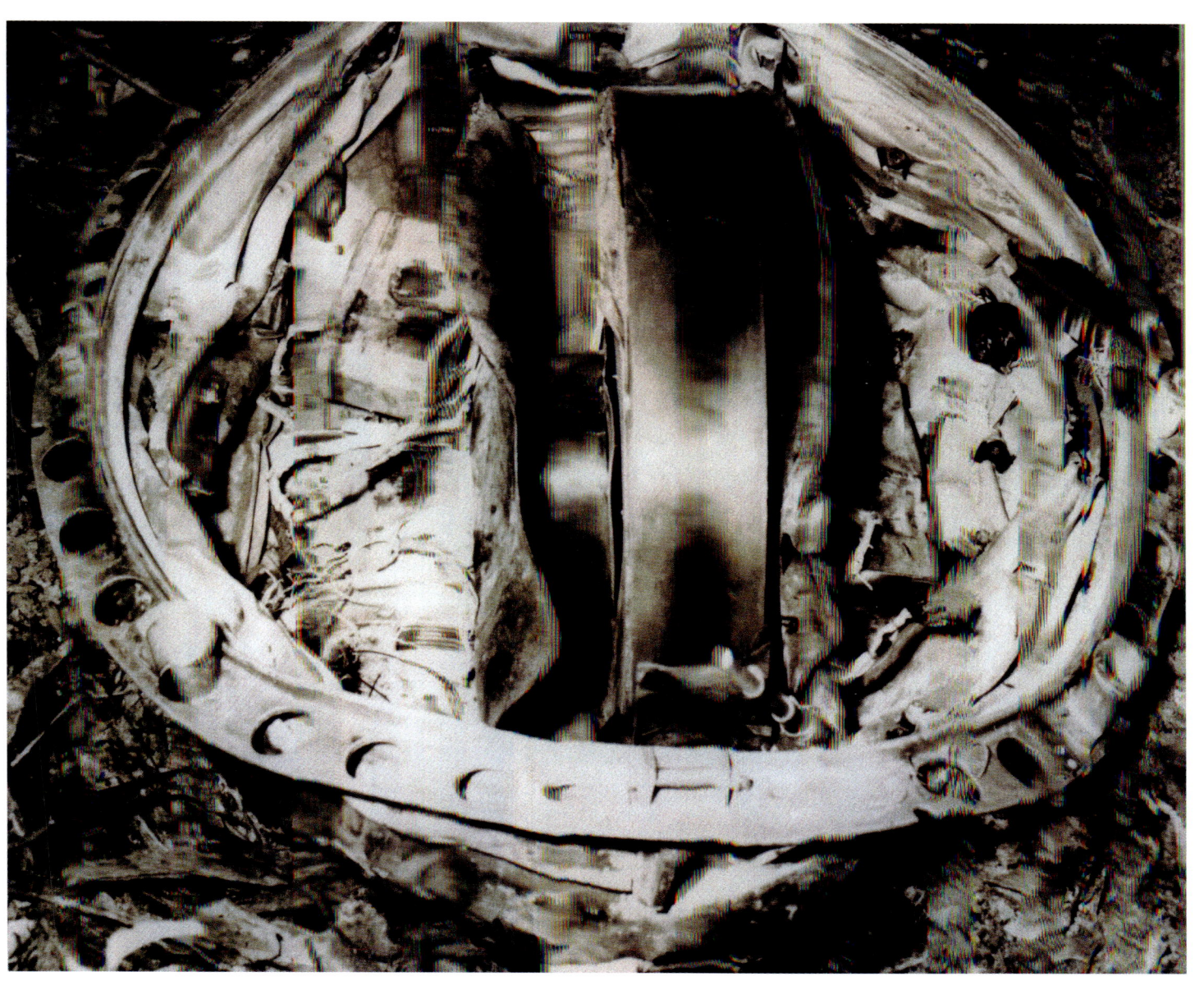

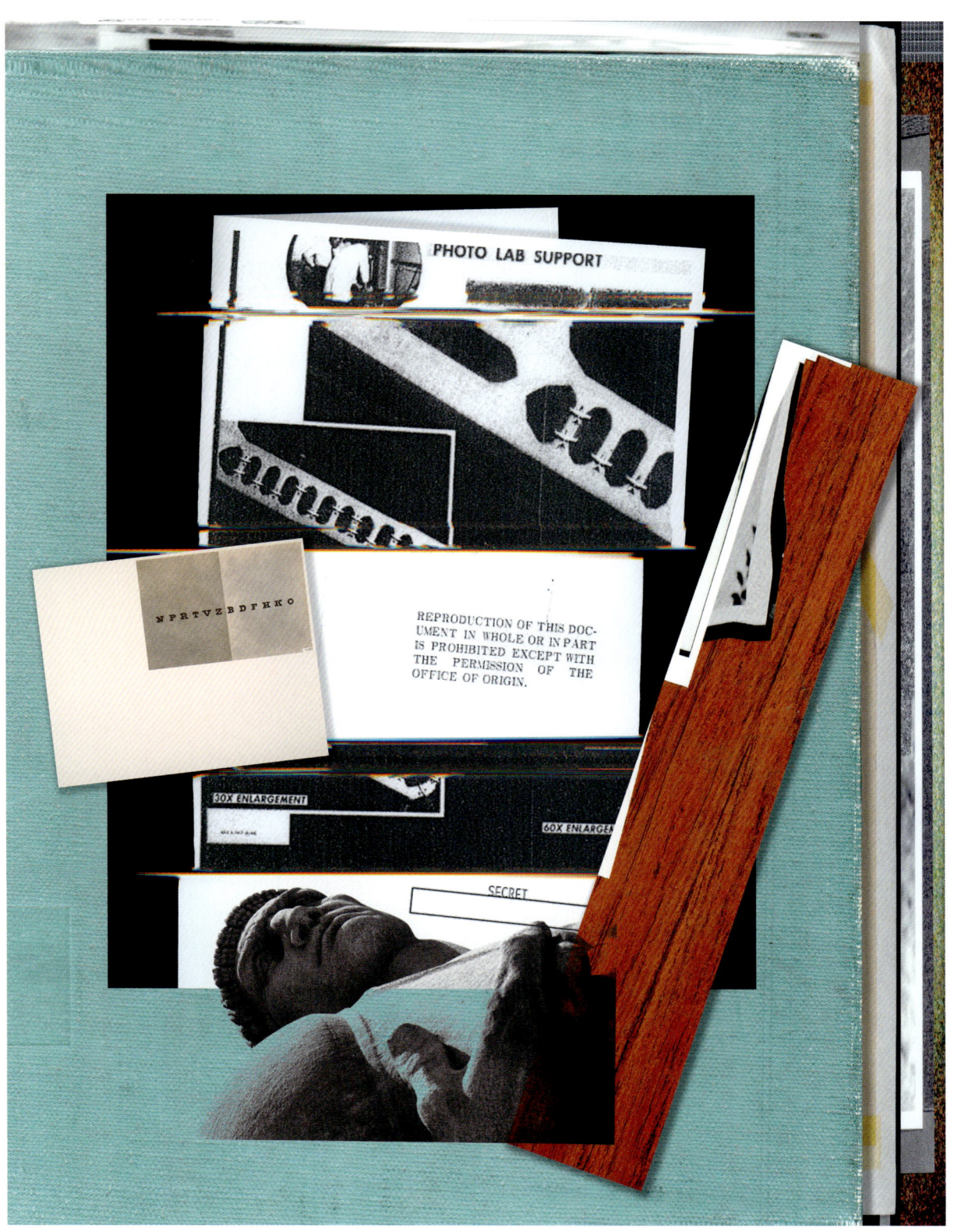

PHOTO LAB SUPPORT

N P R T V Z B D F H K O

REPRODUCTION OF THIS DOC-
UMENT IN WHOLE OR IN PART
IS PROHIBITED EXCEPT WITH
THE PERMISSION OF THE
OFFICE OF ORIGIN.

30X ENLARGEMENT

60X ENLARGEM

SECRET

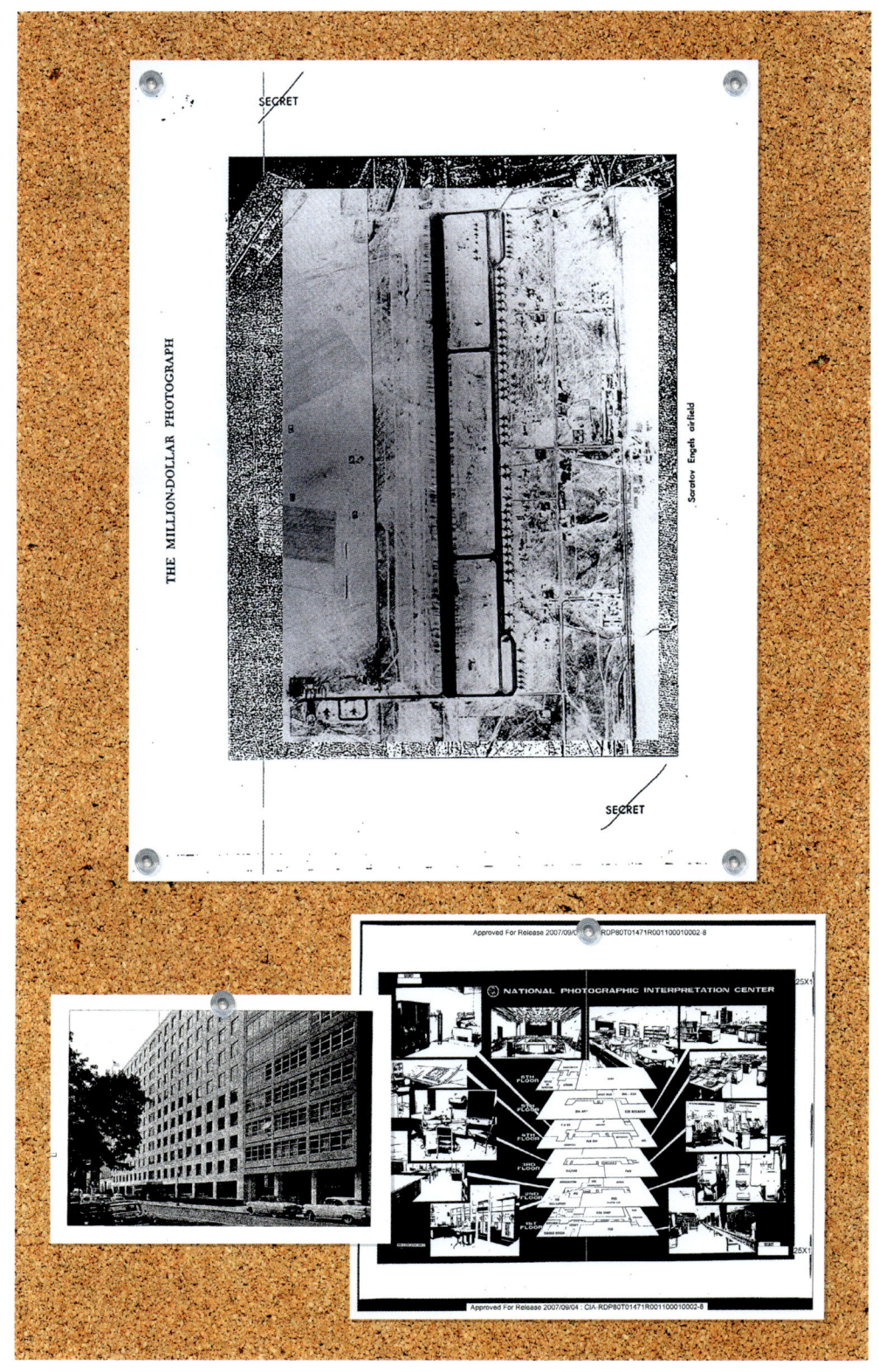

SECRET

THE MILLION-DOLLAR PHOTOGRAPH

Saratov Engels airfield

SECRET

NATIONAL PHOTOGRAPHIC INTERPRETATION CENTER

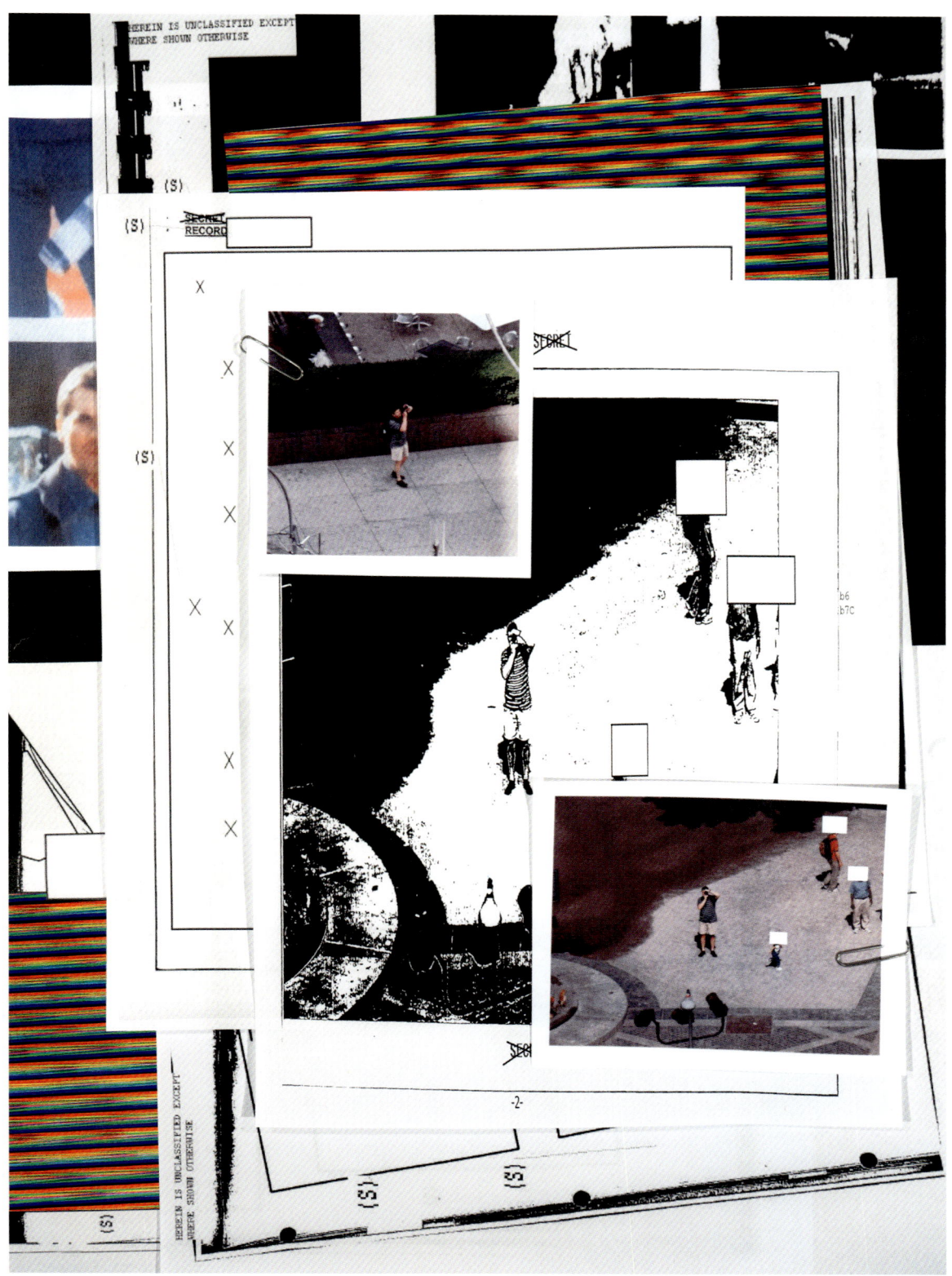

man who manipulates the camera controls, who is responsible for the intermediate photographic processes? The man who establishes the viewpoint of the camera? One viewpoint out of many possible? He is the man who has to make this decision. And many other decisions. And by those decisions we judge him.

He makes his decisions according to what he knows. And in judging his decision we are judging his whole experience, not so much with the camera as with life itself. He may be a rank beginner with the camera, yet if he succeeds in conveying to us a fresh look at the world around us—he has done an important thing.

After all, what is a photographer? Someone who makes photographs not with a retoucher's brush and knife, but with a camera. Why does he make photographs? Because he wants to show us something we cannot get around to seeing for ourselves. And because he wants to show it to us *the way he saw it.* We call a photographer good, when he shows us something that interests us or attracts our attention. That may be a locomotive, if we are railroad hobbyists, or races, if we are fond of the track, or chorus girls, new roads, steam shovels, sewage disposal plants, billboards, sharecroppers or soldiers in action. Interests of the human being are great and varied, and the variety of these interests is what gives photography its significance.

Photography, considered as a means to record a mere likeness, is not very difficult. But photography as a new method in the age-old struggle of the human being to

whether the subject is a single person or a large group, a city block or a whole region of the country. It is necessary to understand people, how and where they live, what they do at work or at their leisure, what they have done to their environment, and what that environment has done to them.

If the subject is small in scale, understanding may be derived at first hand, from direct observation. If large, observations of others, the economic geographer, the historian, the sociologist—must be called upon. The photographer should allow no limitations to restrict his research, except that of time. In no other way will his work stand out under a test of time. Mere technical excellence can be equalled and surpassed by others almost overnight, but work based upon knowledge and understanding of the subject and of the world surrounding it will always have an honored place, not only in photographic exhibition, but whenever things of interest to people are sought. The photographer speaks through his camera, and the importance of what he has to say is limited only by his ability to express himself in terms of the language of photography and his own knowledge of the world. His task, difficult but rewarding, is to live up to the full possibilities of his medium.

However, only those who master the mechanics of photography can afford to "forget it." Mastery of the mechanics of photography is, at best, only a means to an end. Idolatry of photographic technique has never produced its masterpieces. Neither has the ability to draw

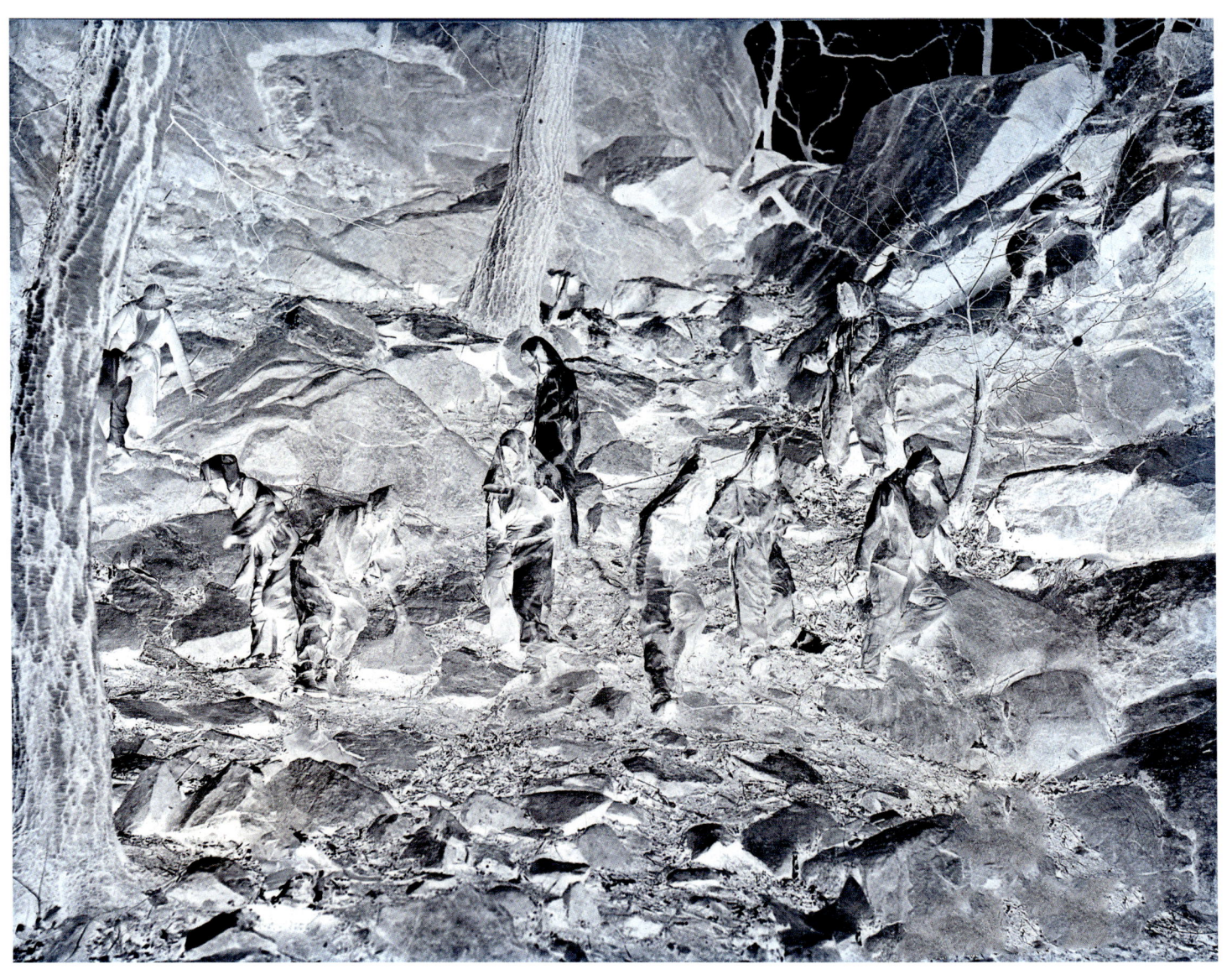

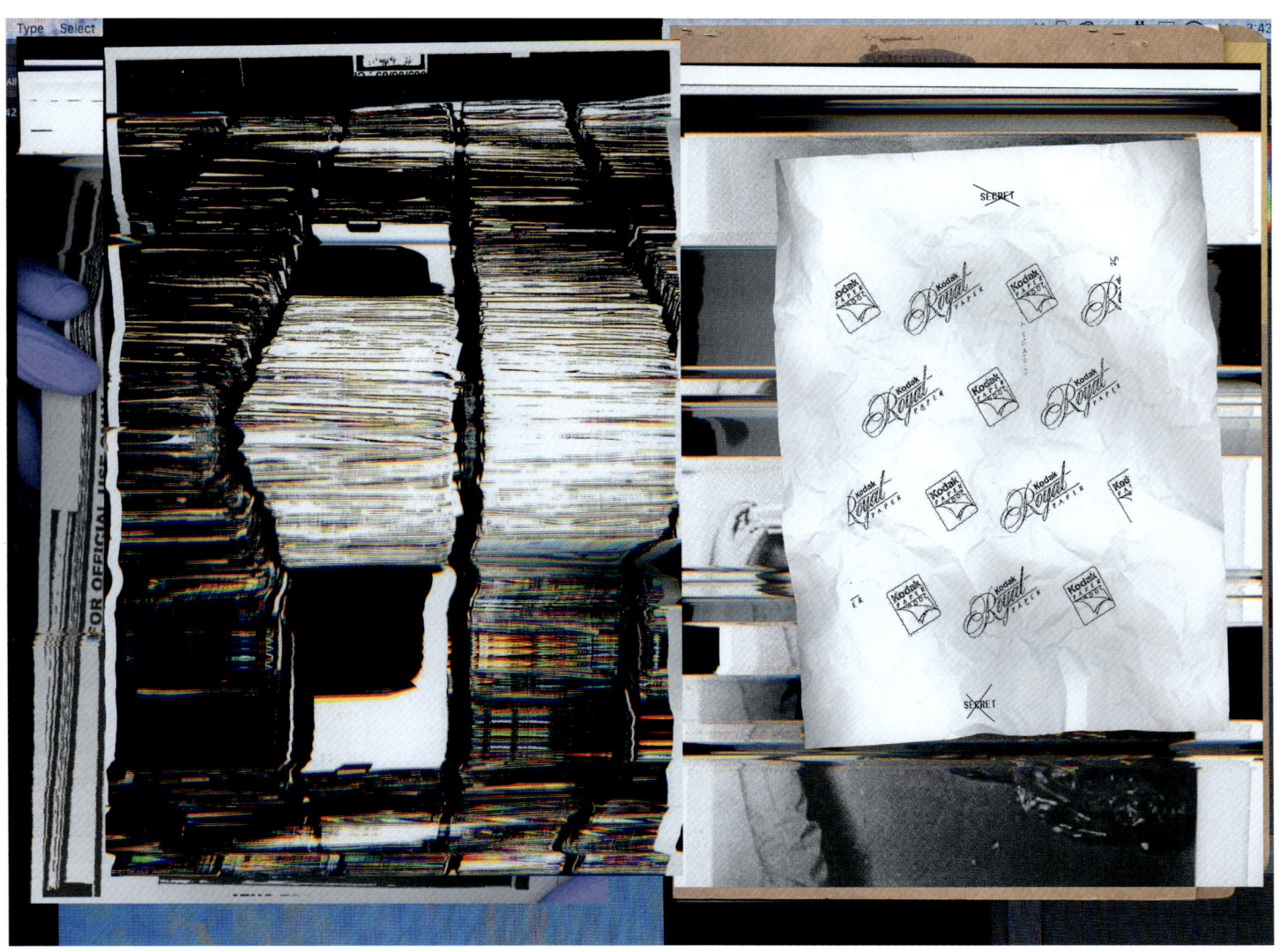

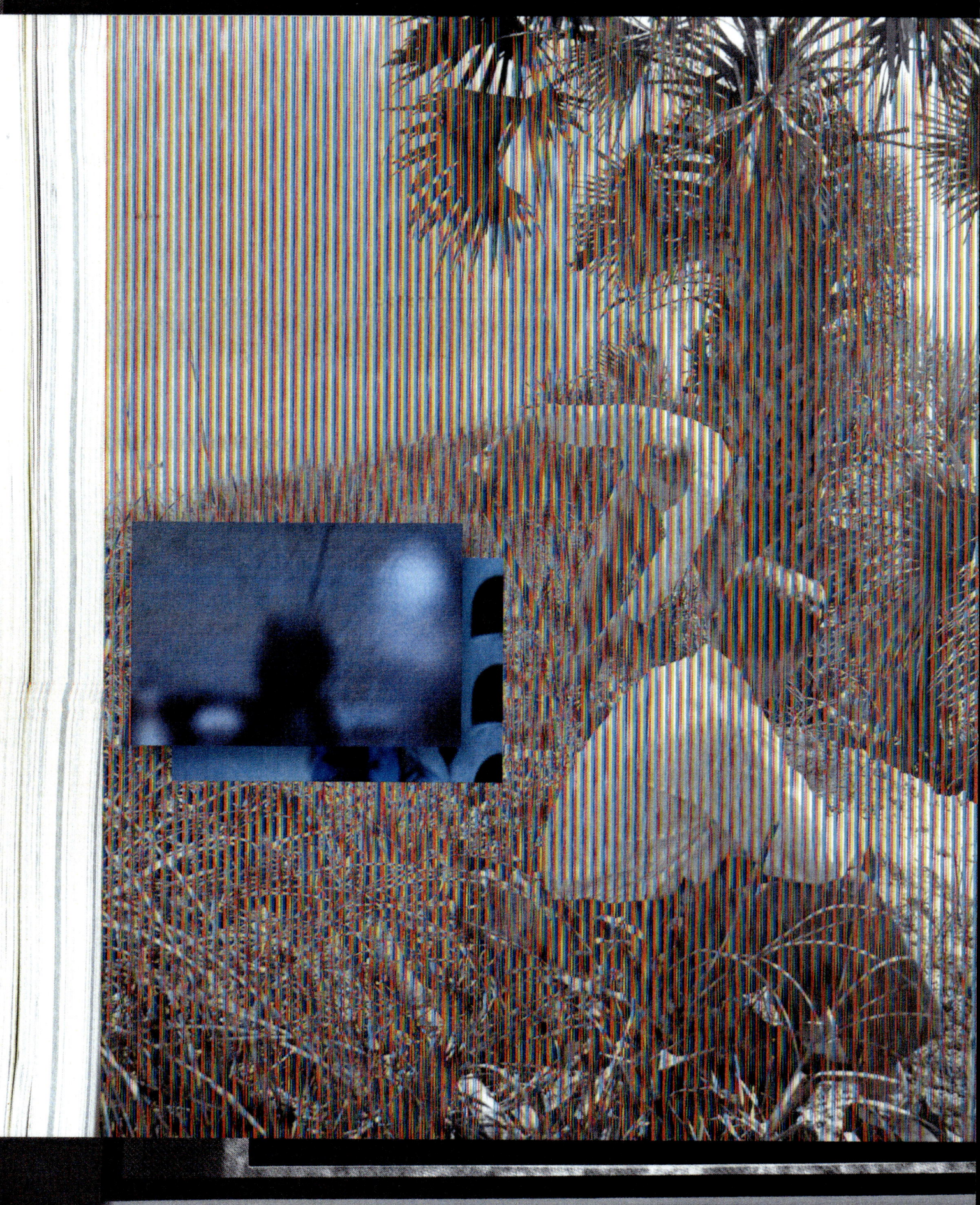

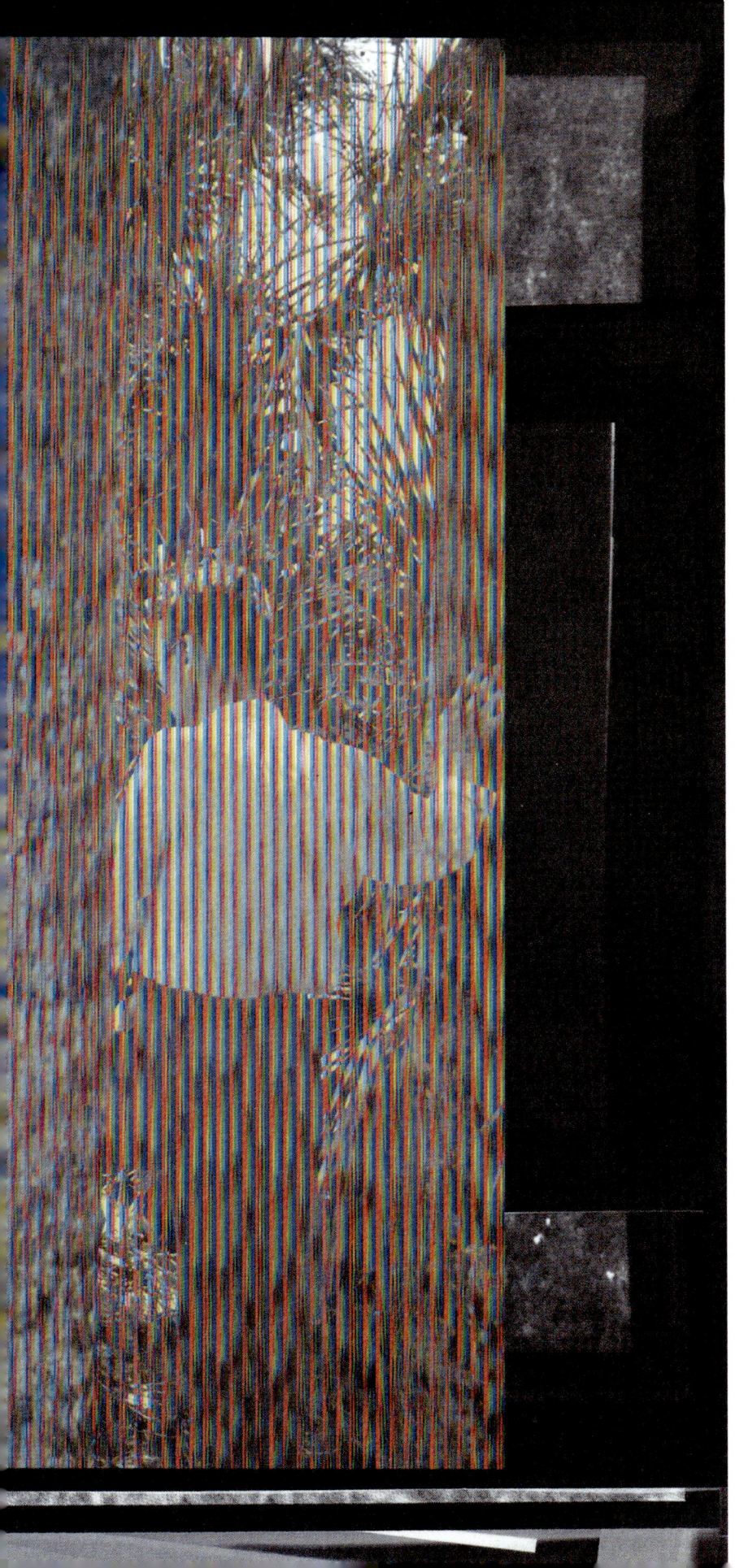

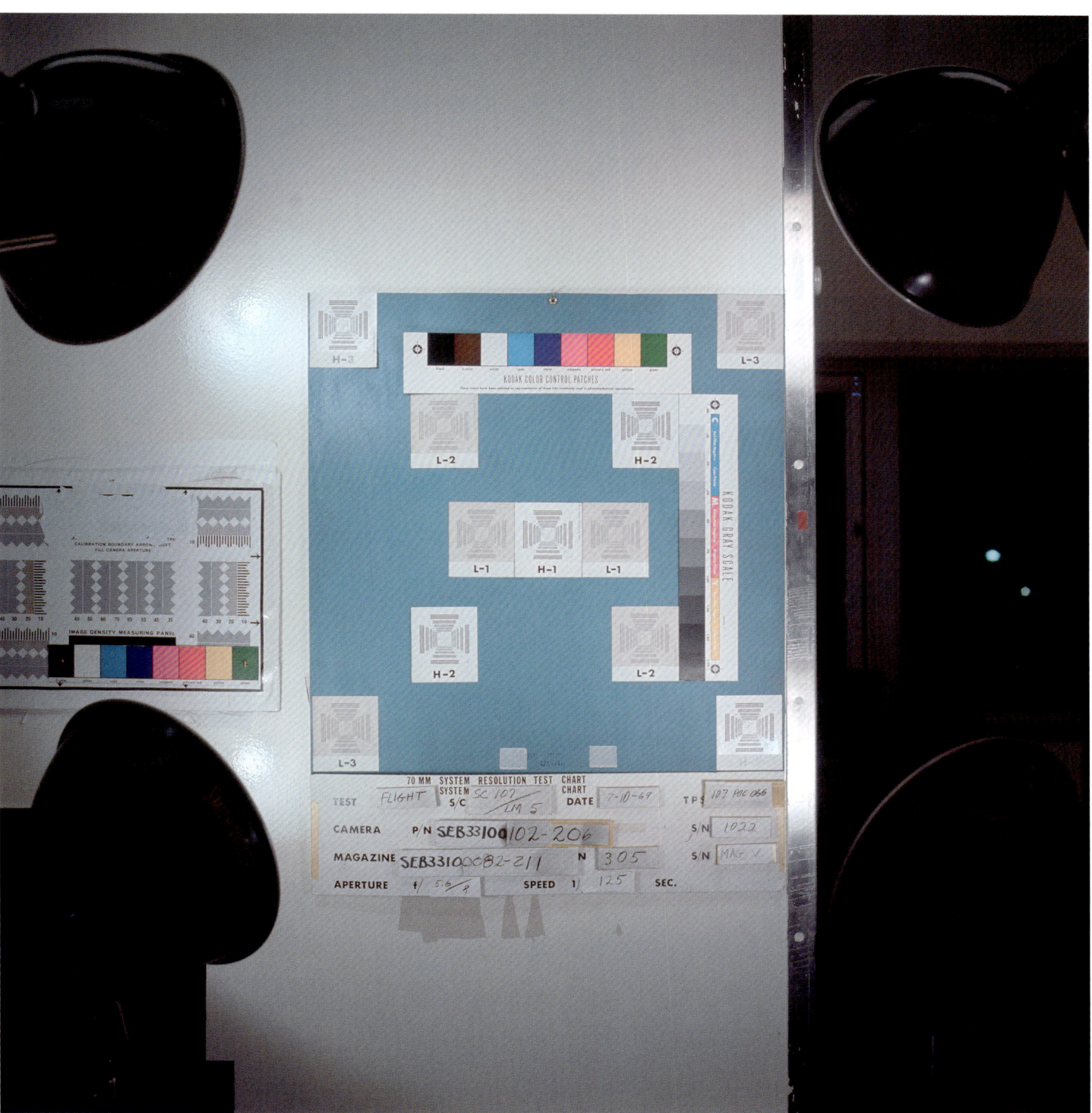

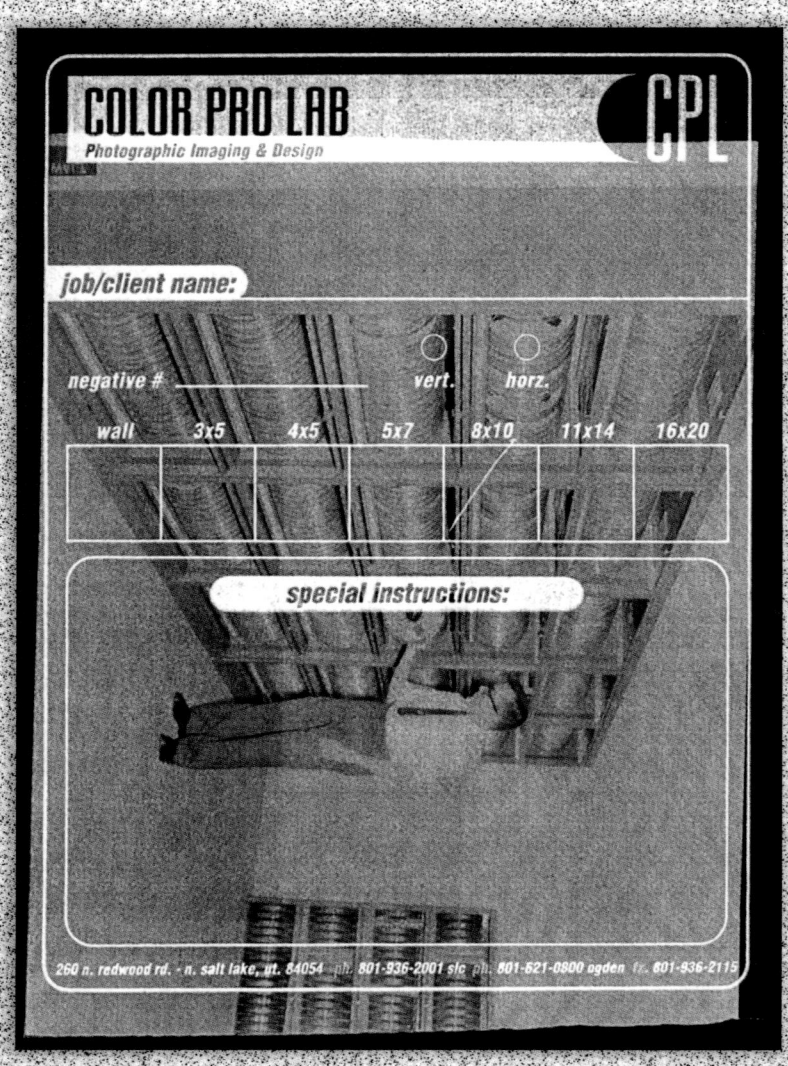

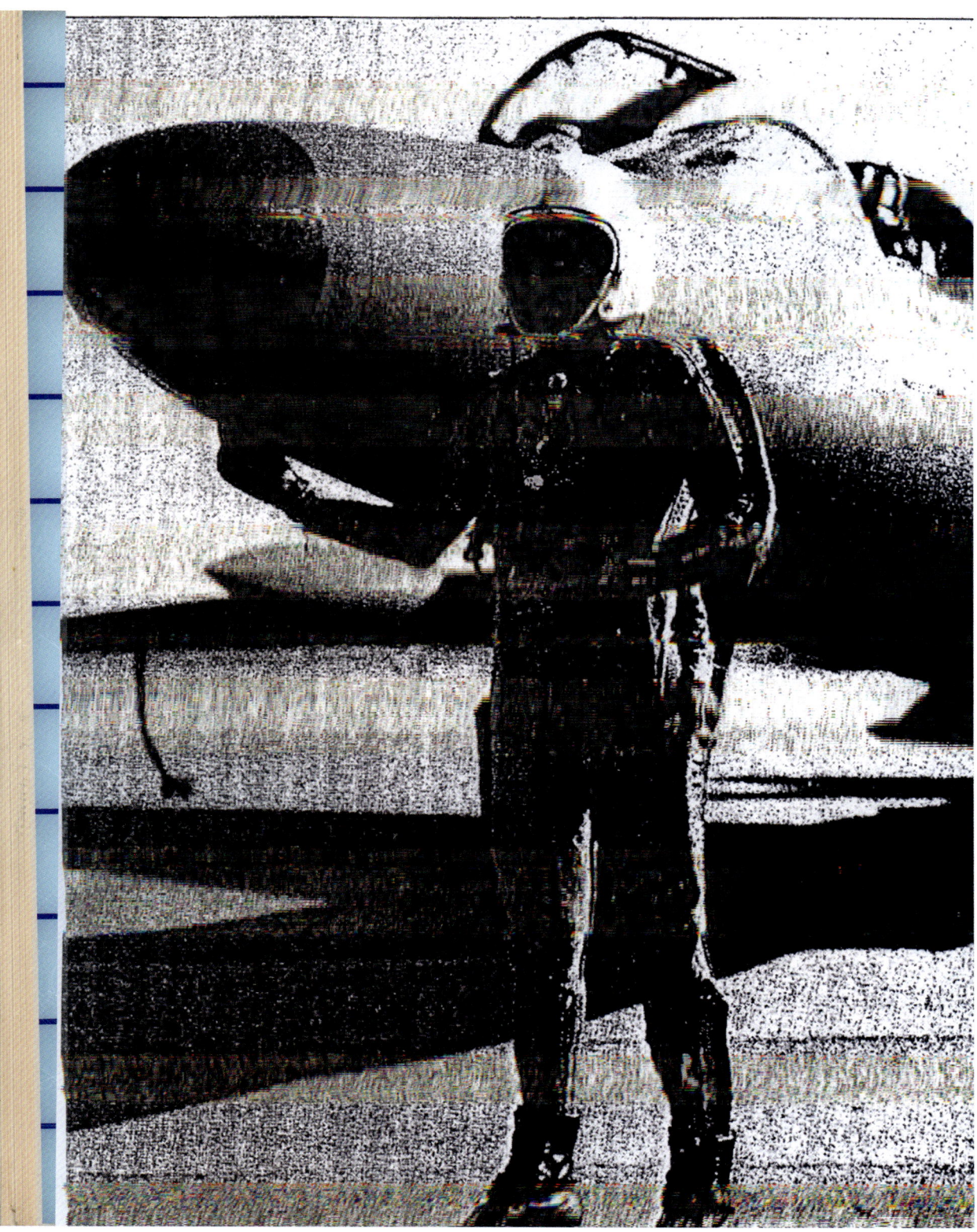

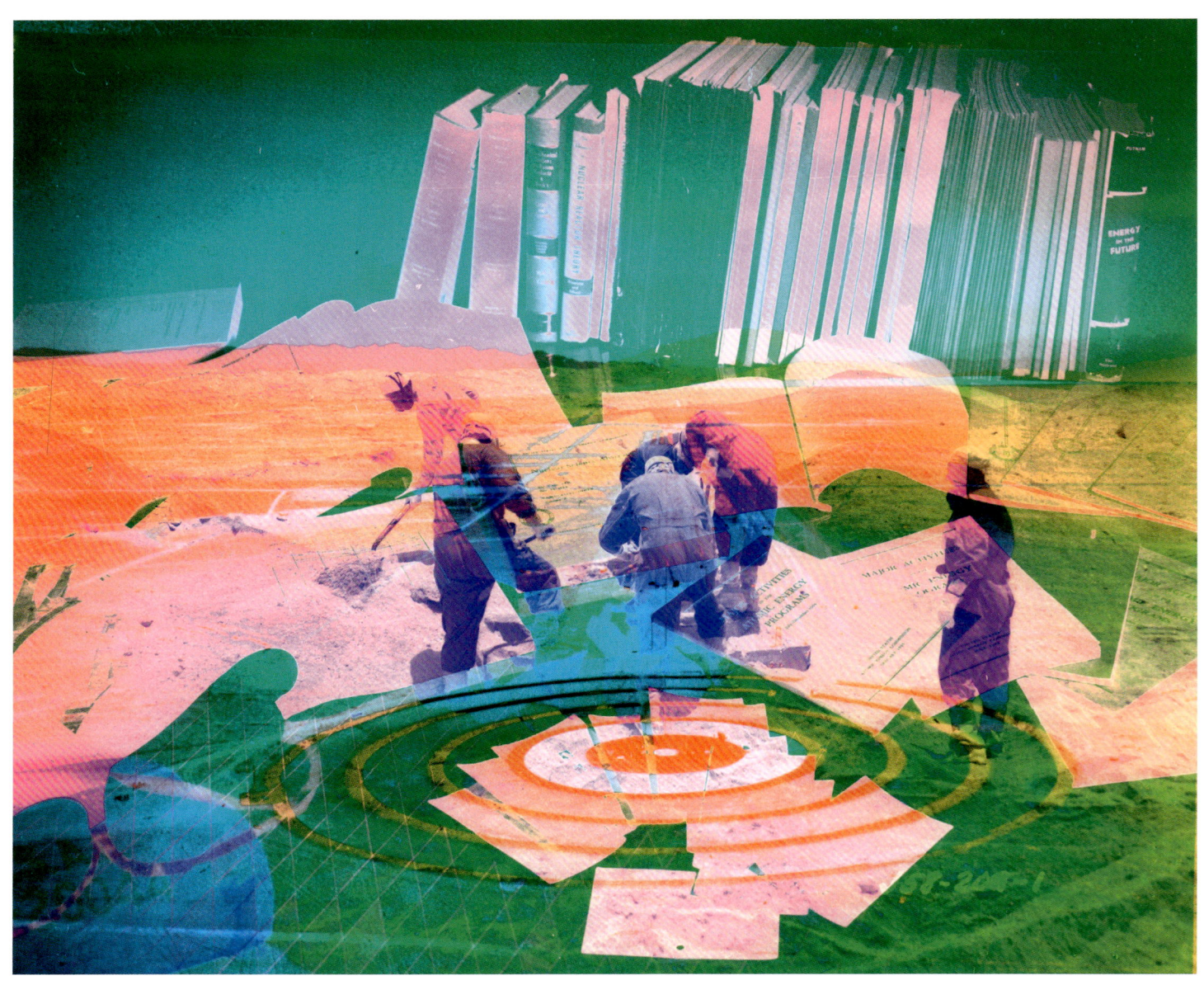

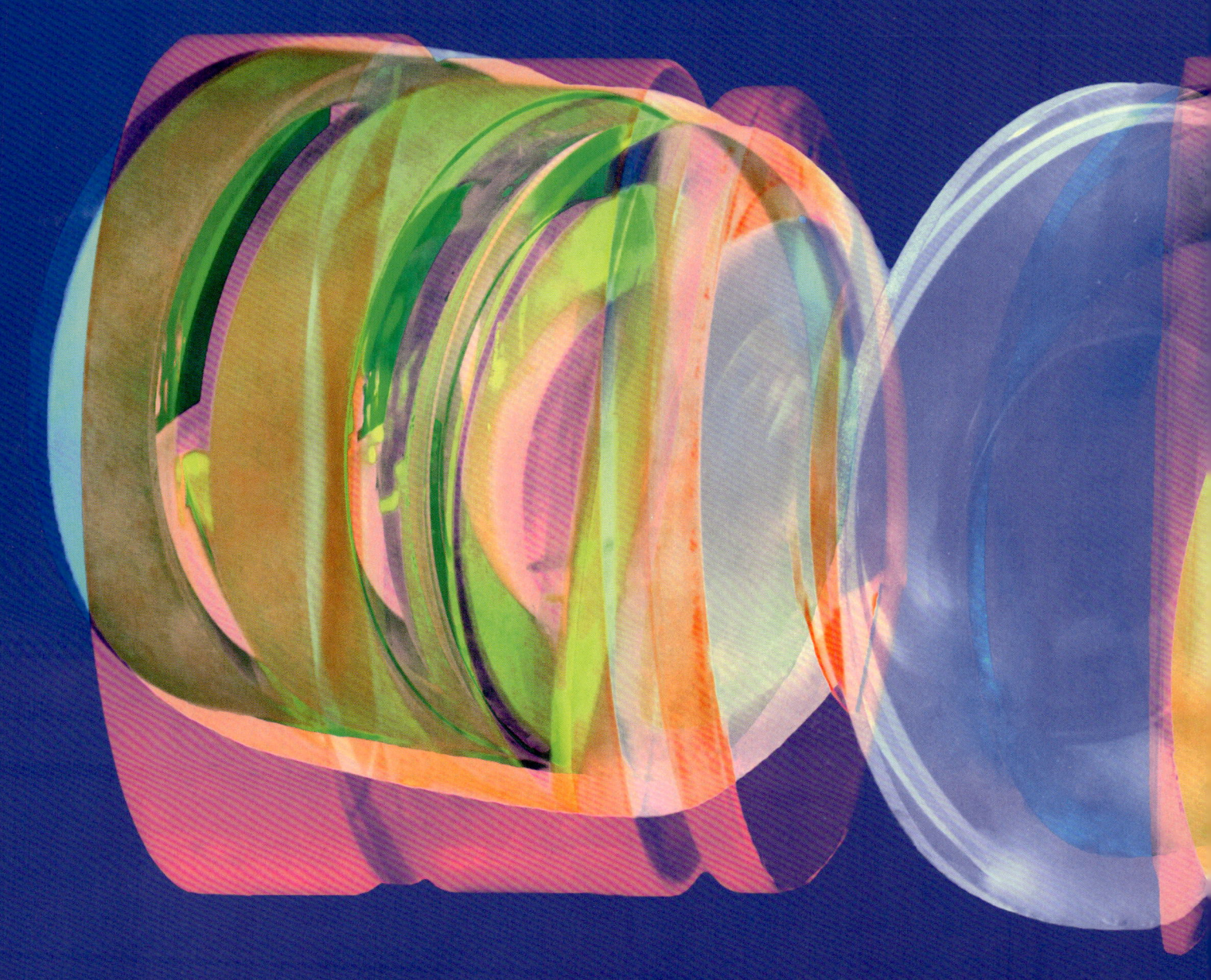

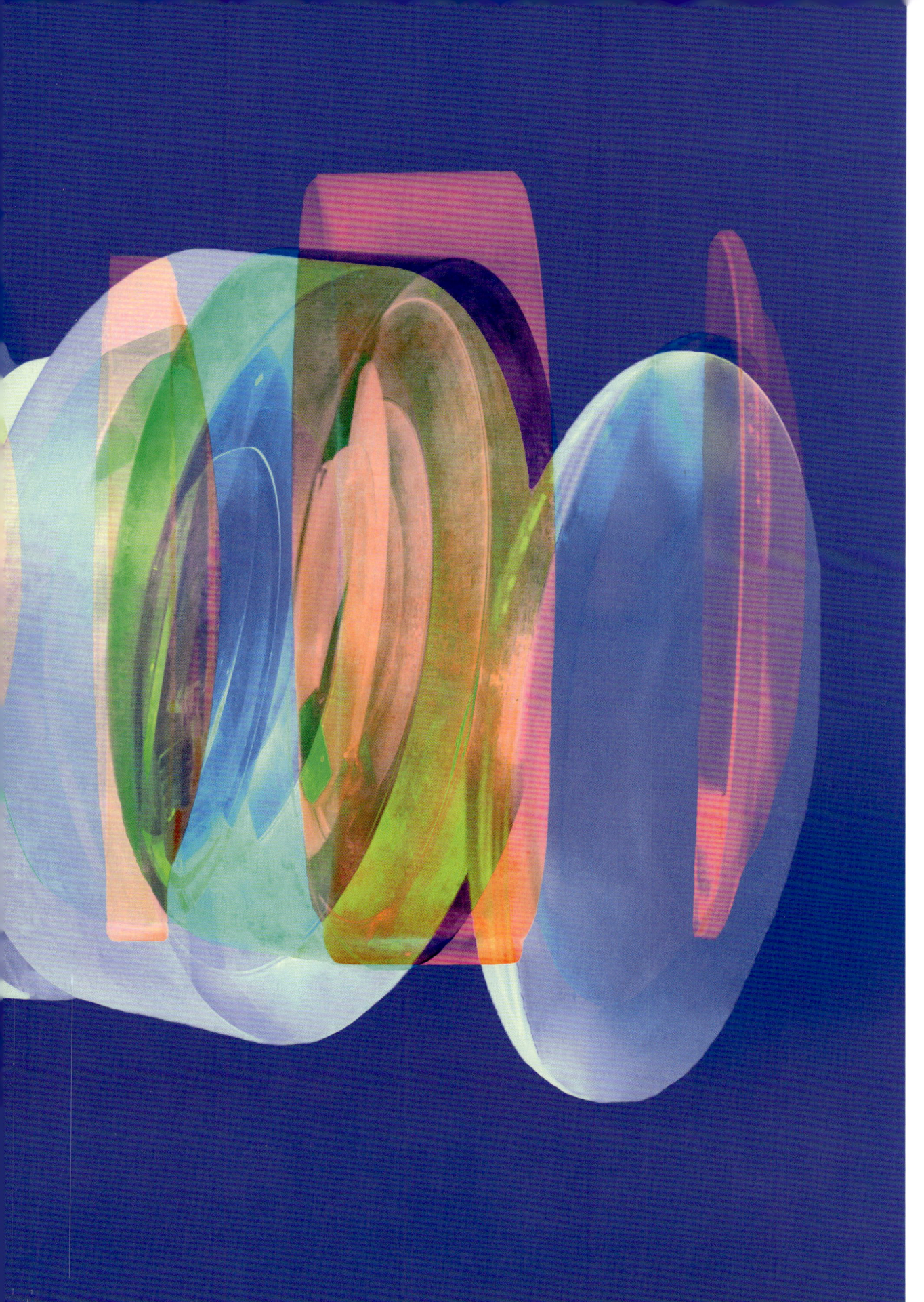

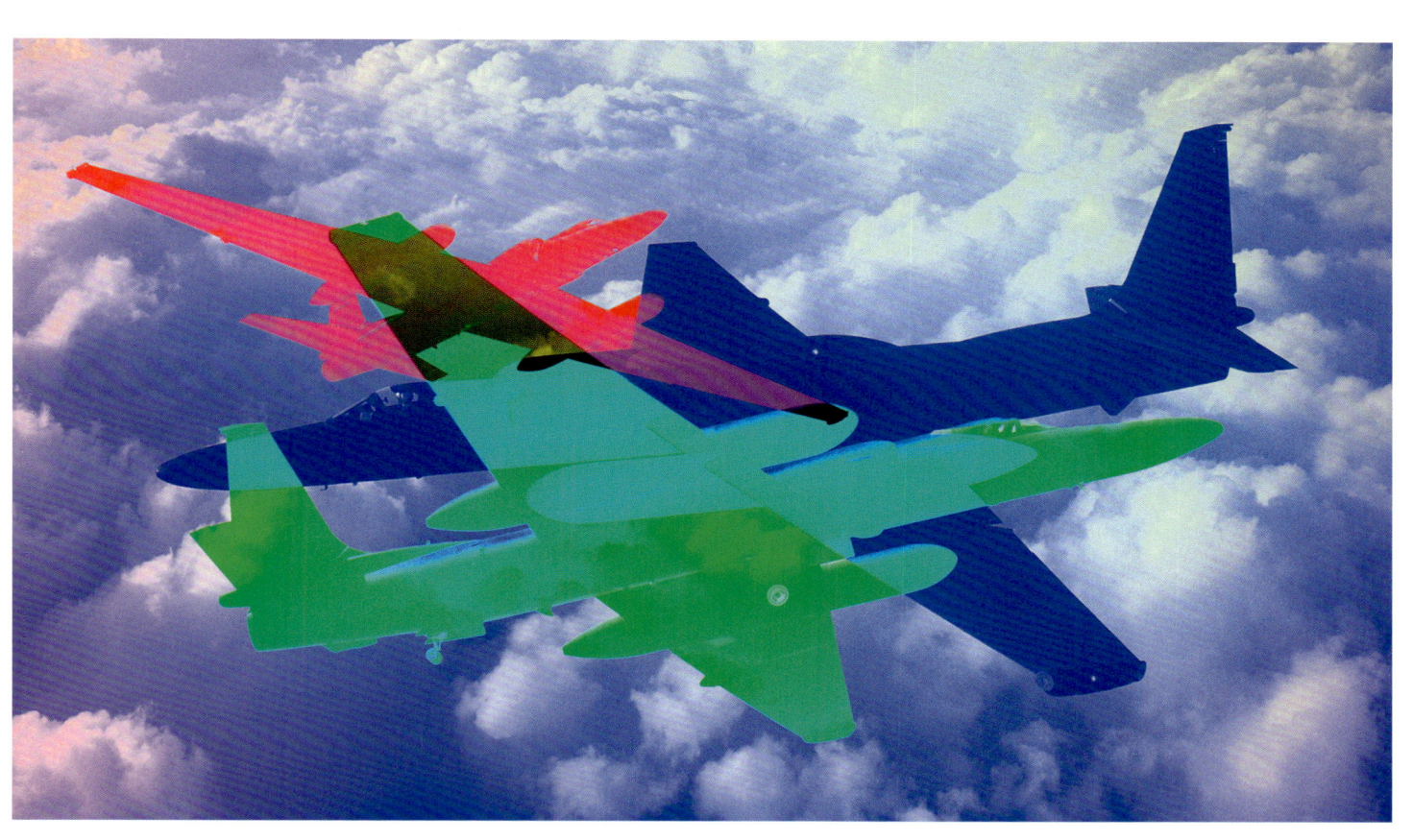

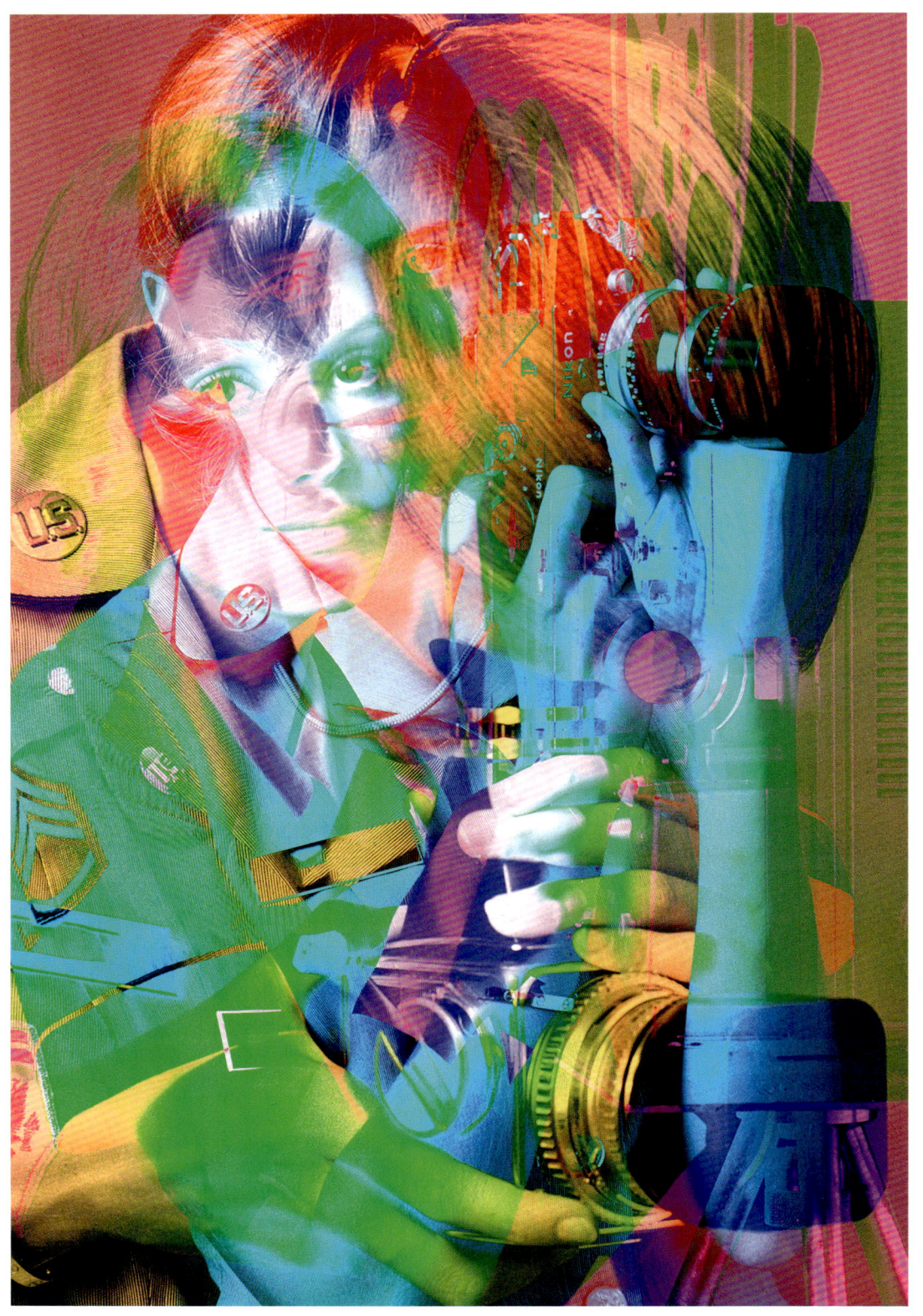

VD_72

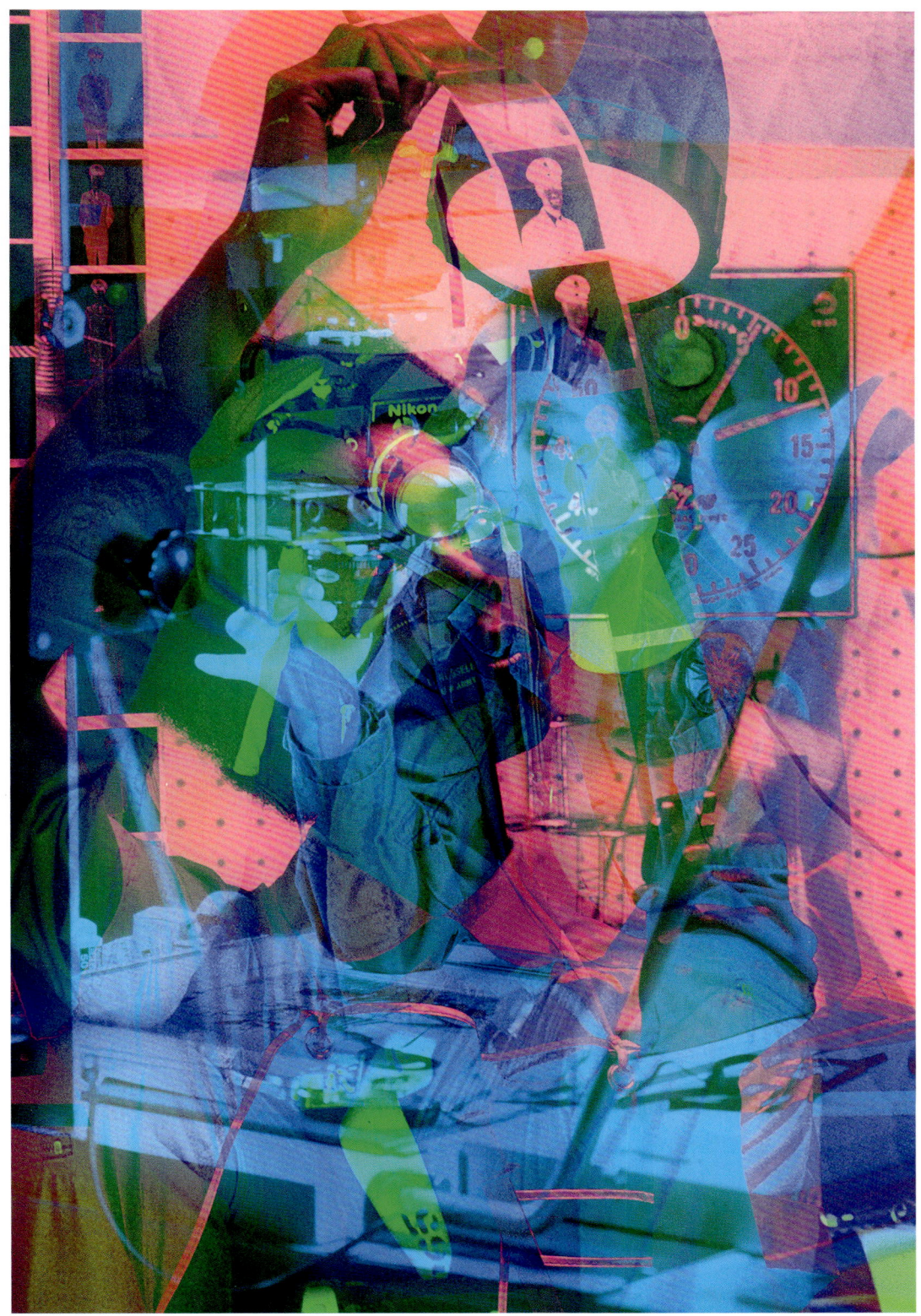

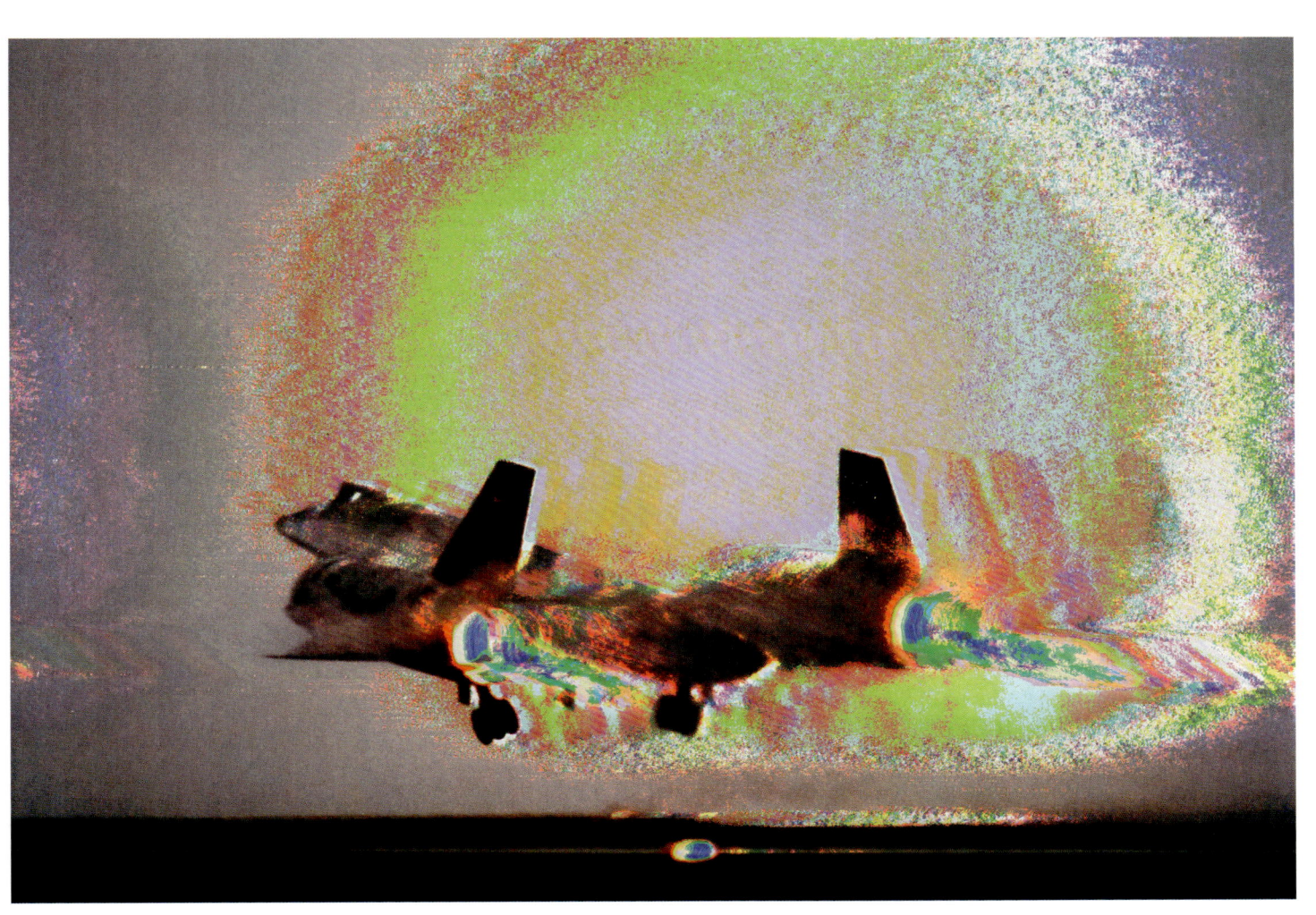

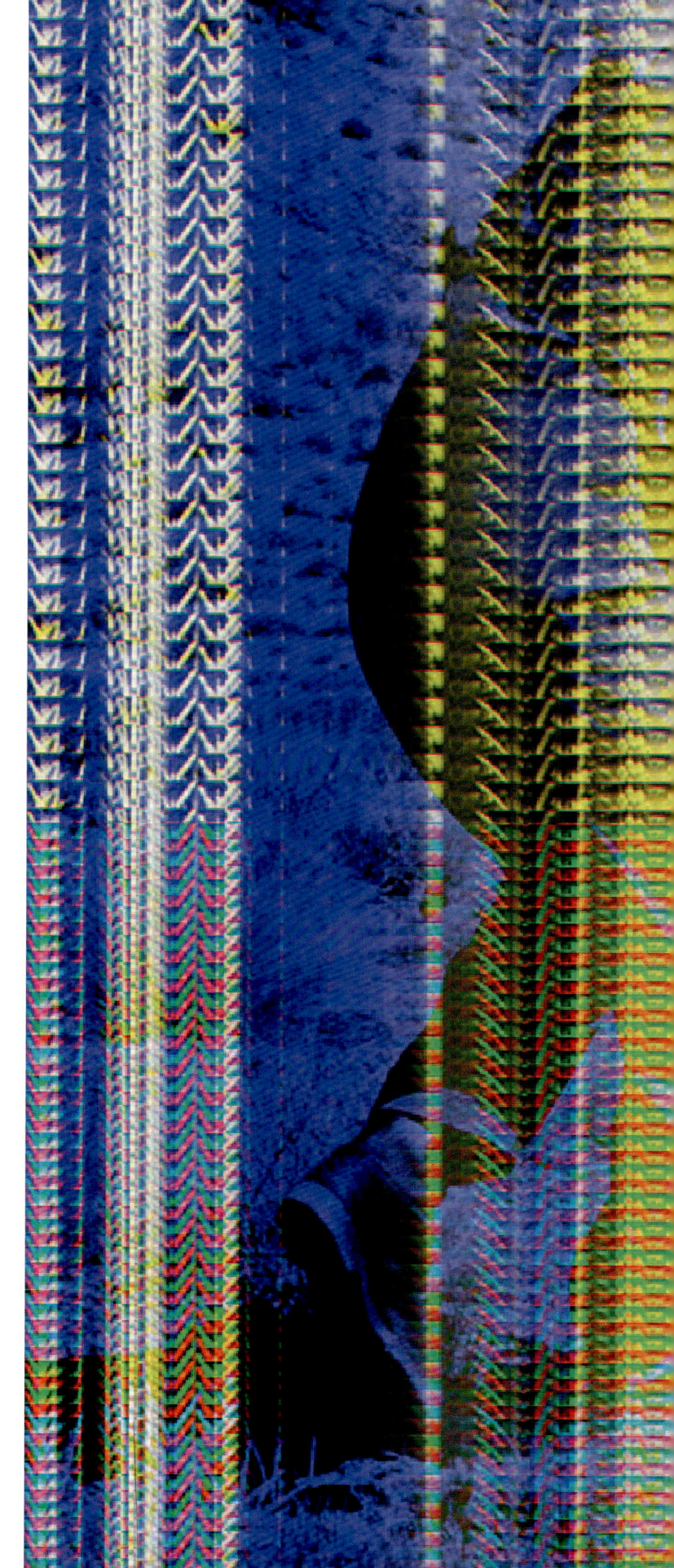

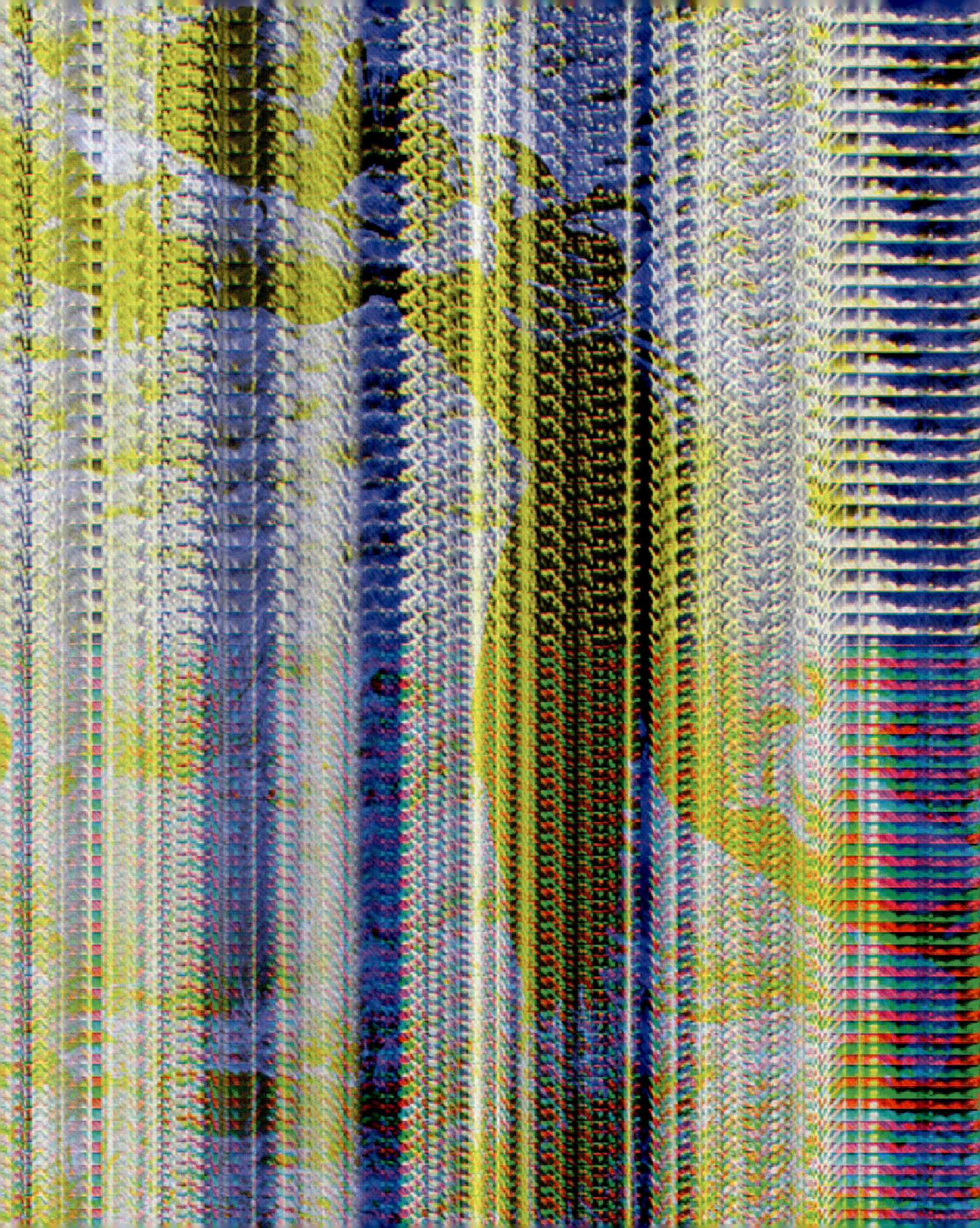

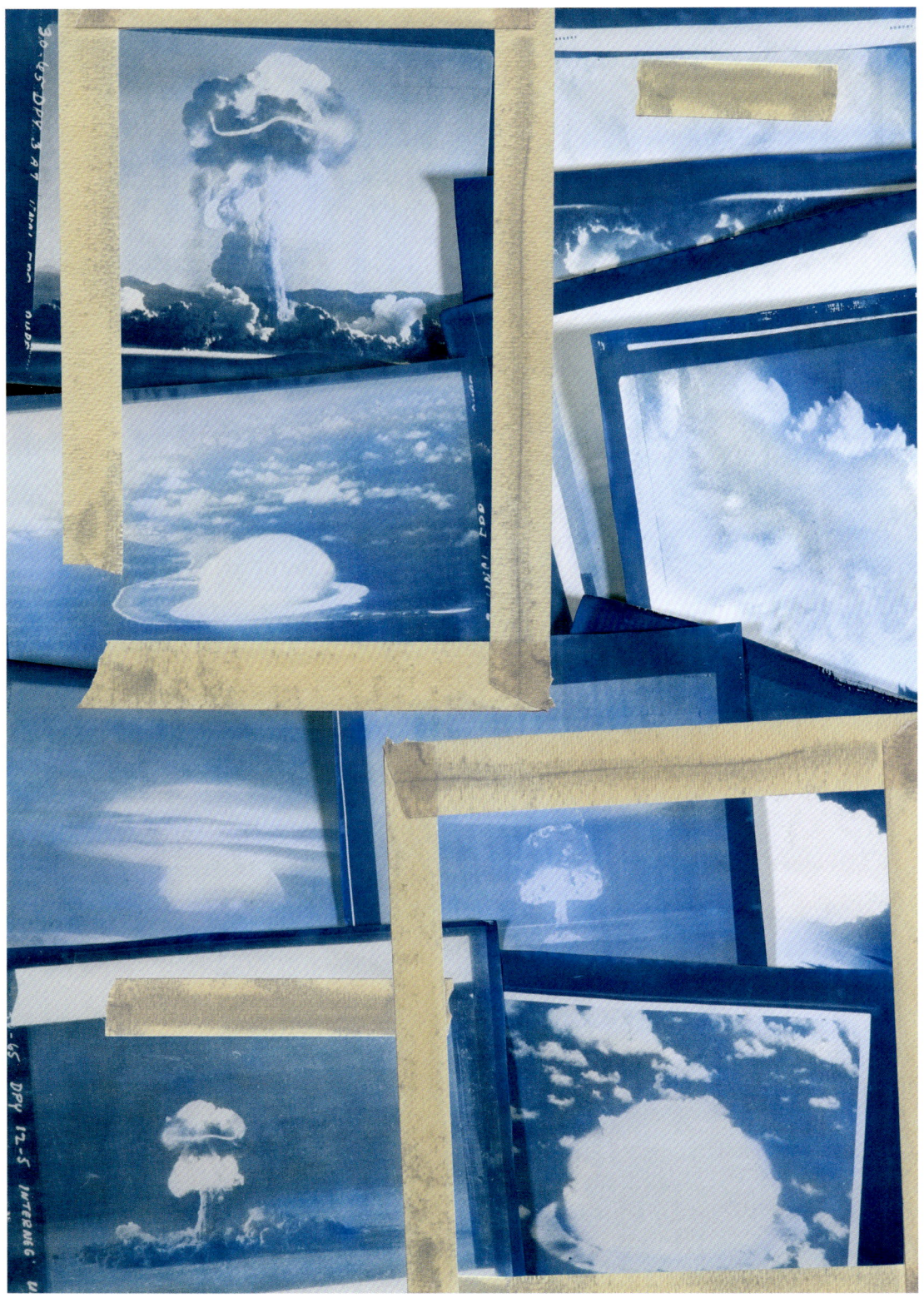

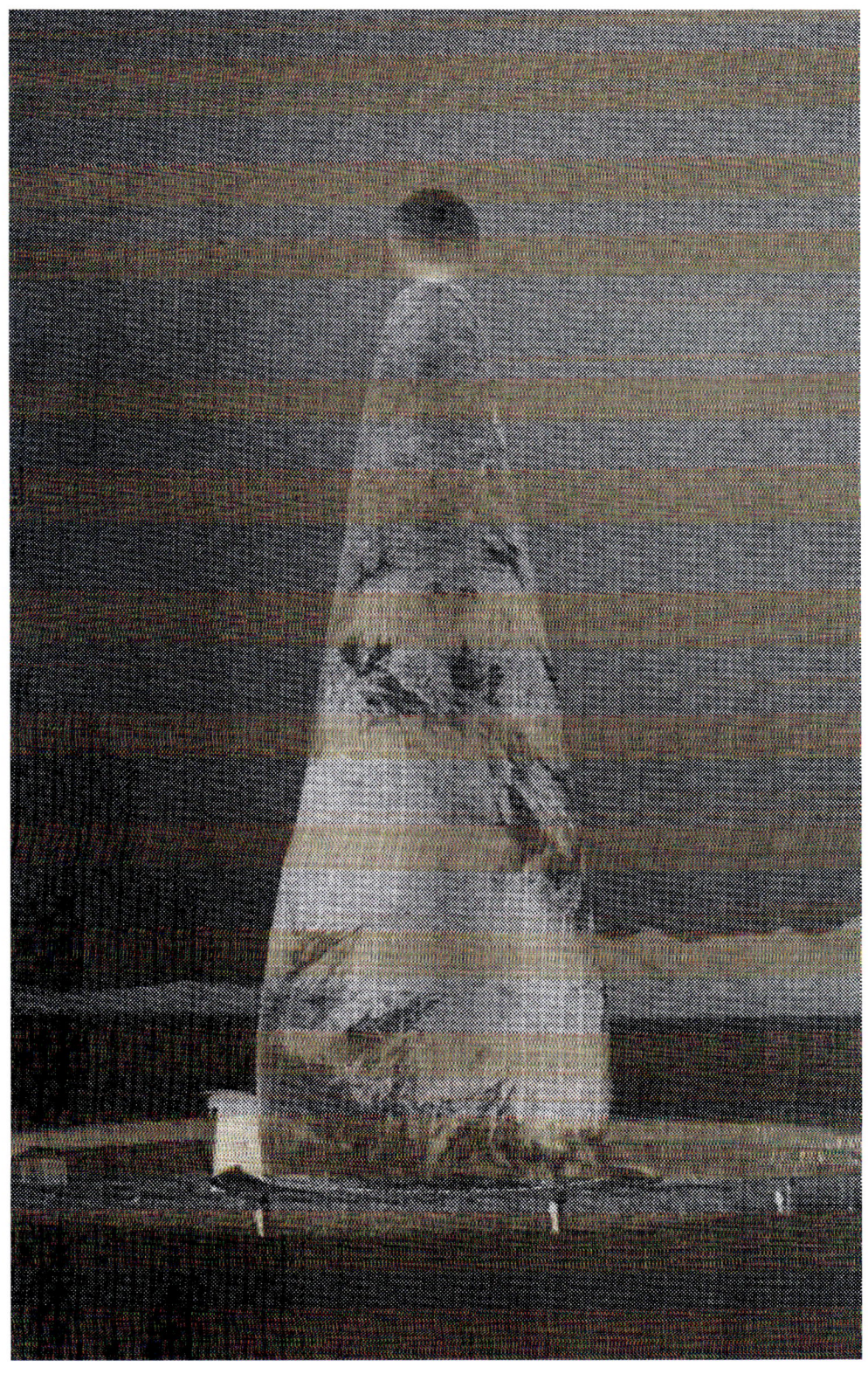

~~SECRET//SI/TK//REL TO USA, FVEY~~

This page consist of (b)(1) and (b)(3) redactions.

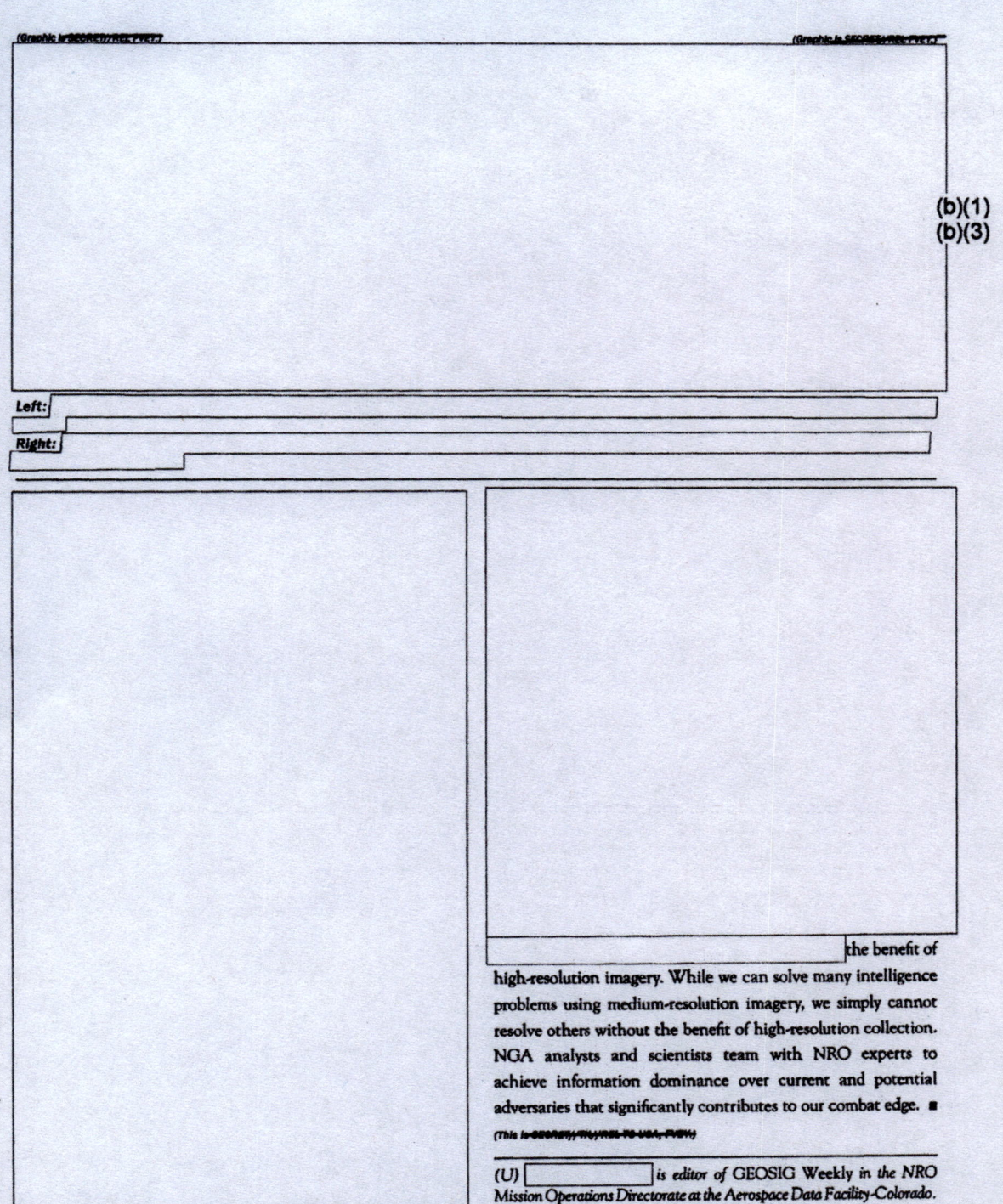

(b)(1)
(b)(3)

Left:

Right:

the benefit of high-resolution imagery. While we can solve many intelligence problems using medium-resolution imagery, we simply cannot resolve others without the benefit of high-resolution collection. NGA analysts and scientists team with NRO experts to achieve information dominance over current and potential adversaries that significantly contributes to our combat edge. ∎

(This is SECRET//TK//REL TO USA, FVEY)

(U) [ ] is editor of GEOSIG Weekly in the NRO Mission Operations Directorate at the Aerospace Data Facility-Colorado.

~~SECRET//SI/TK//REL TO USA, FVEY~~

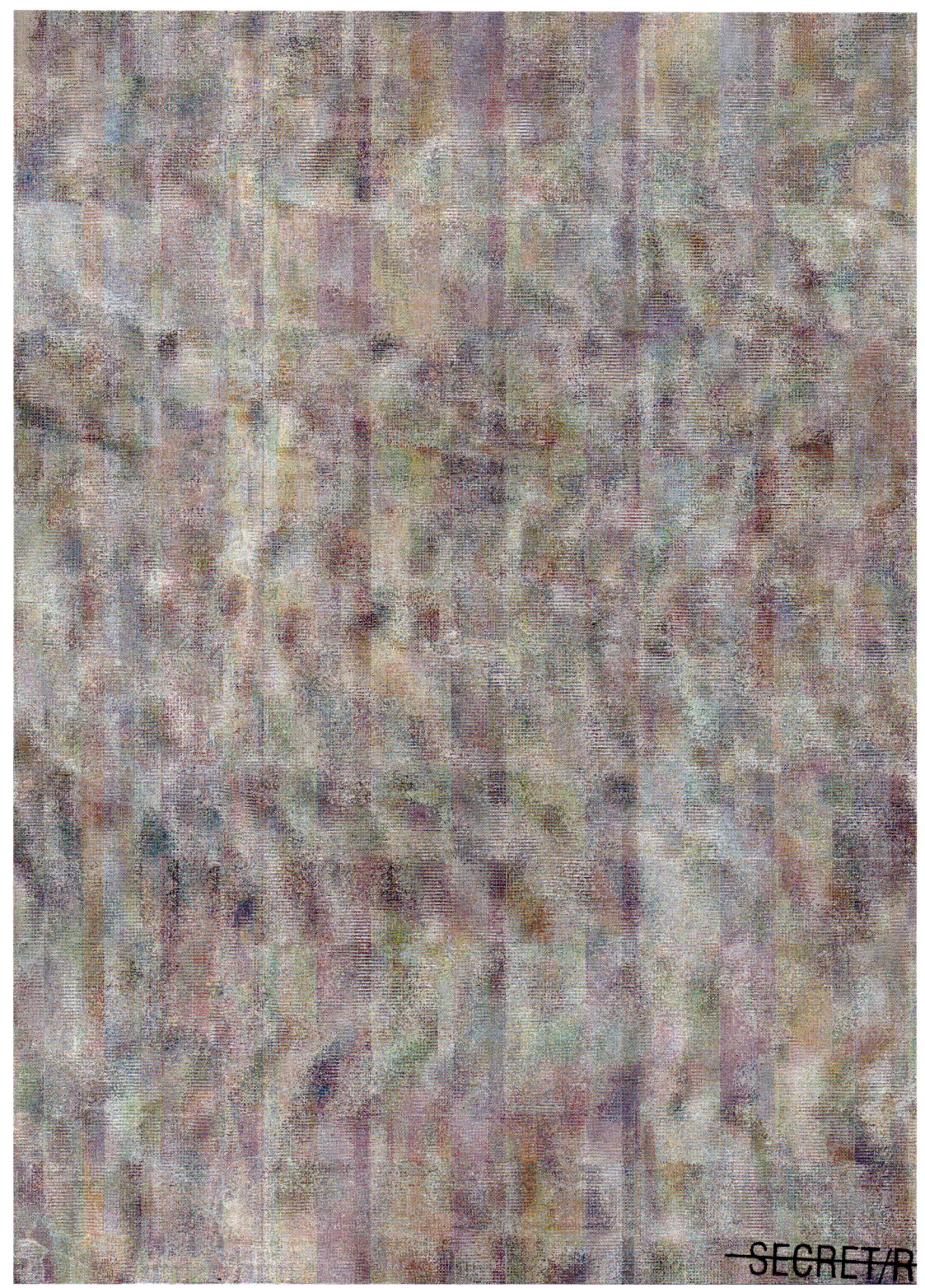

VD_ 81

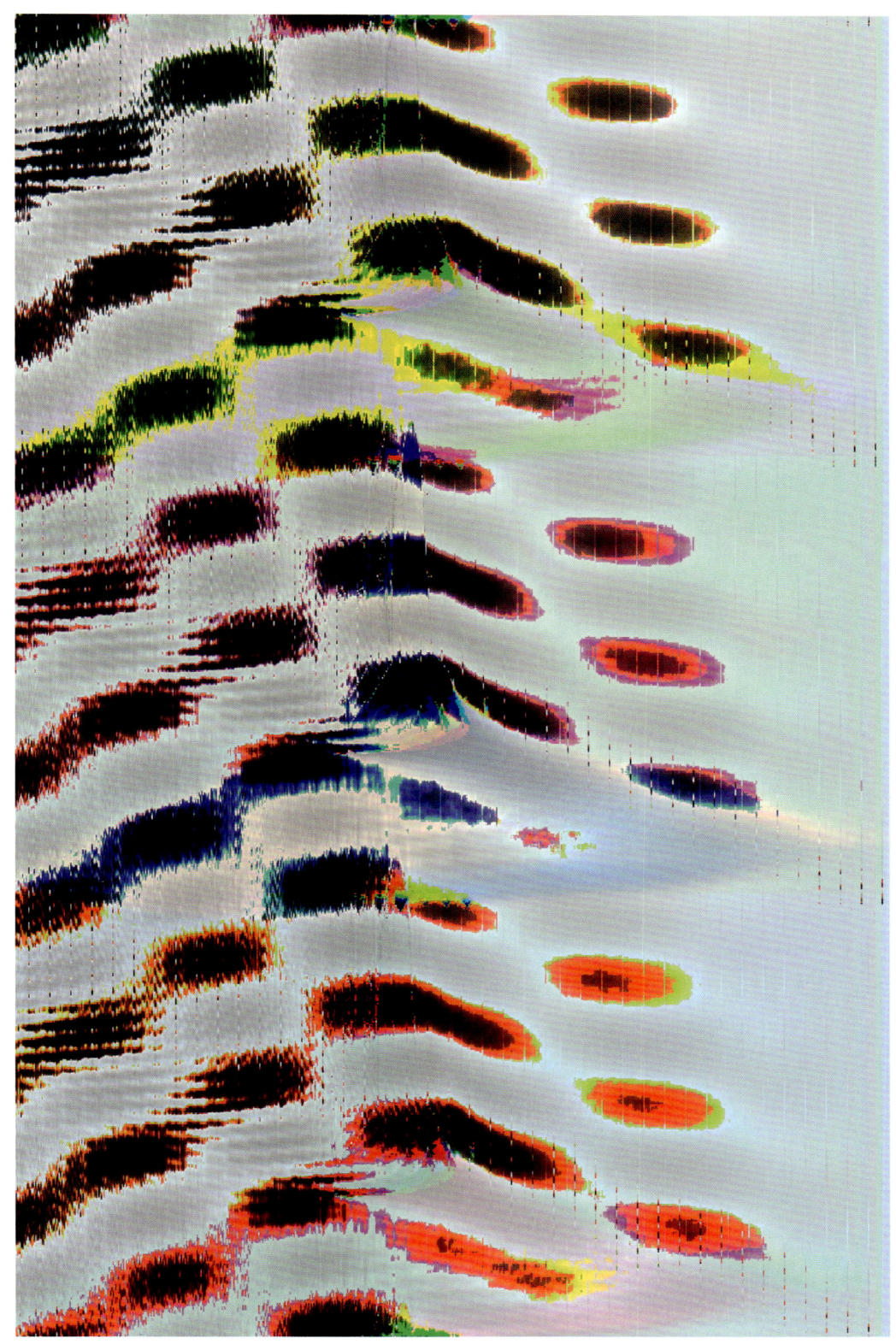

VD_ 83

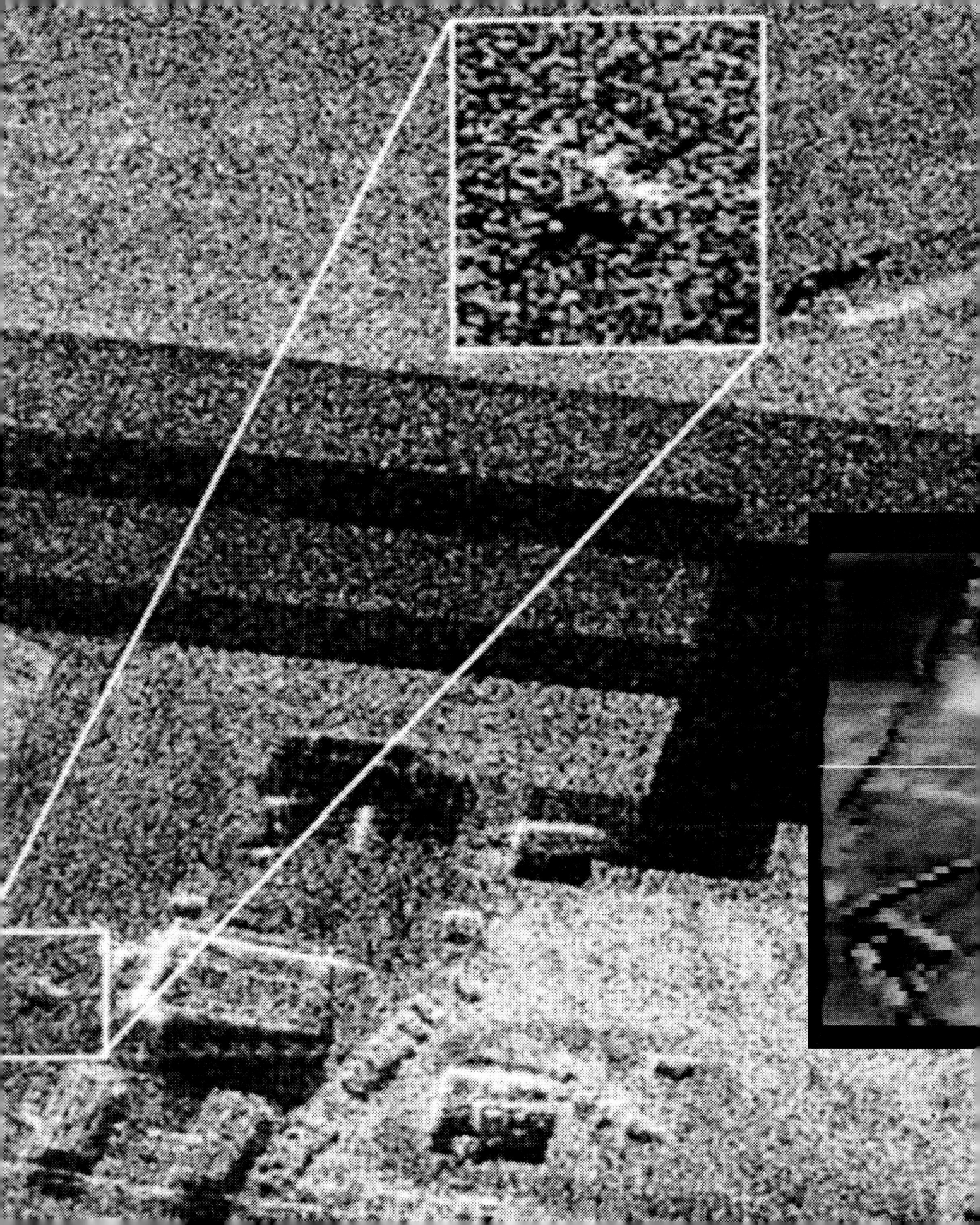

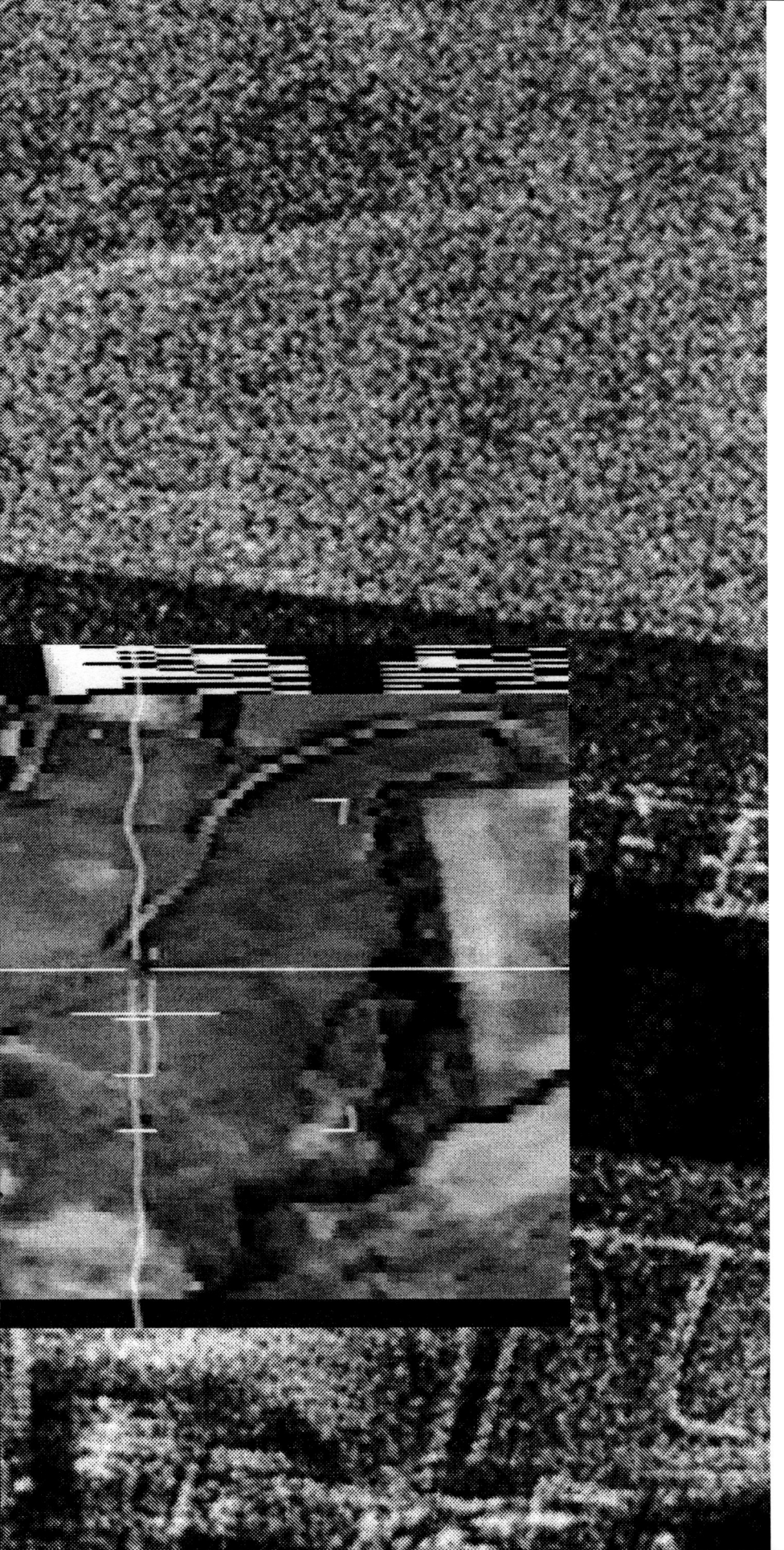

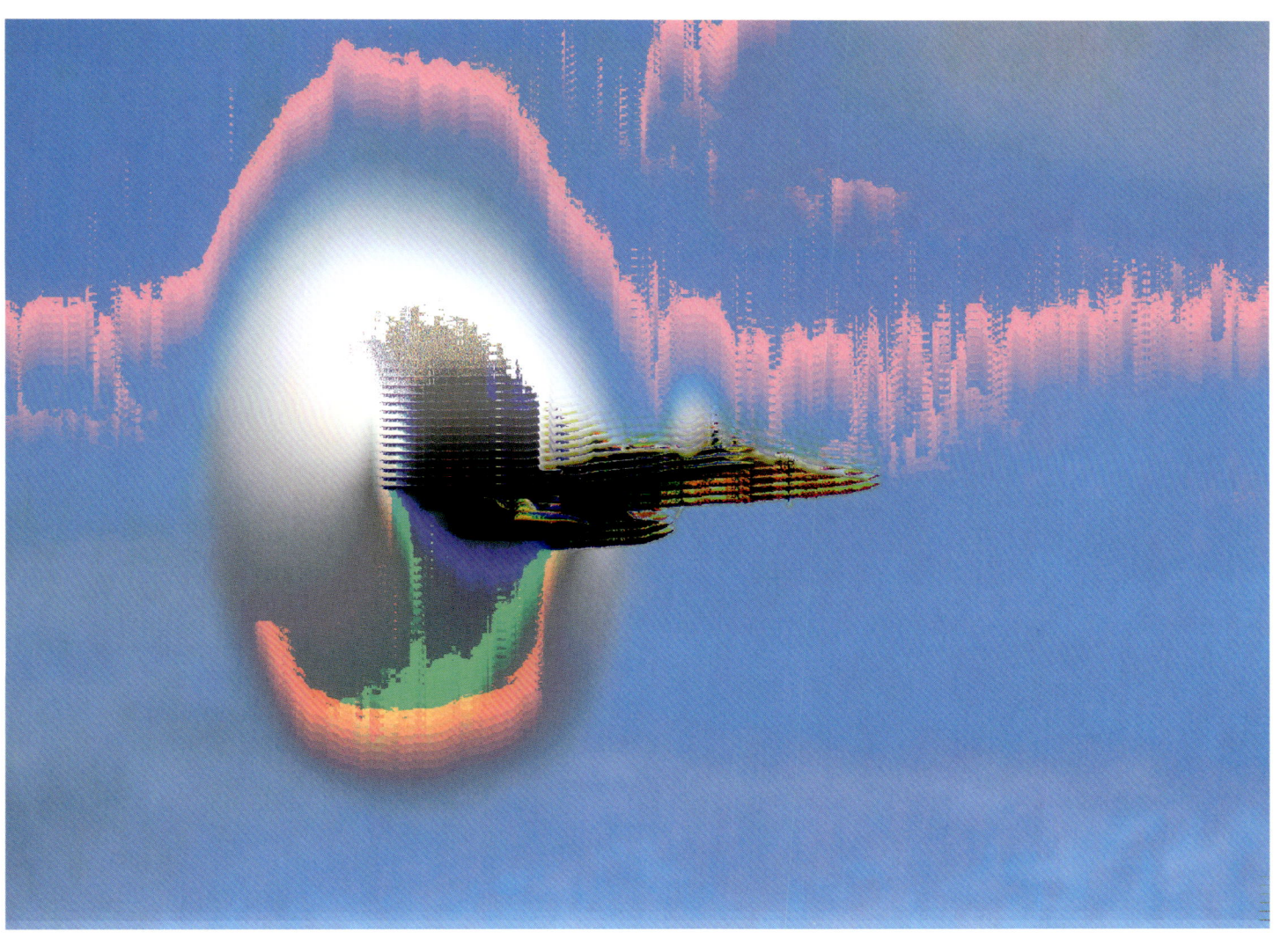

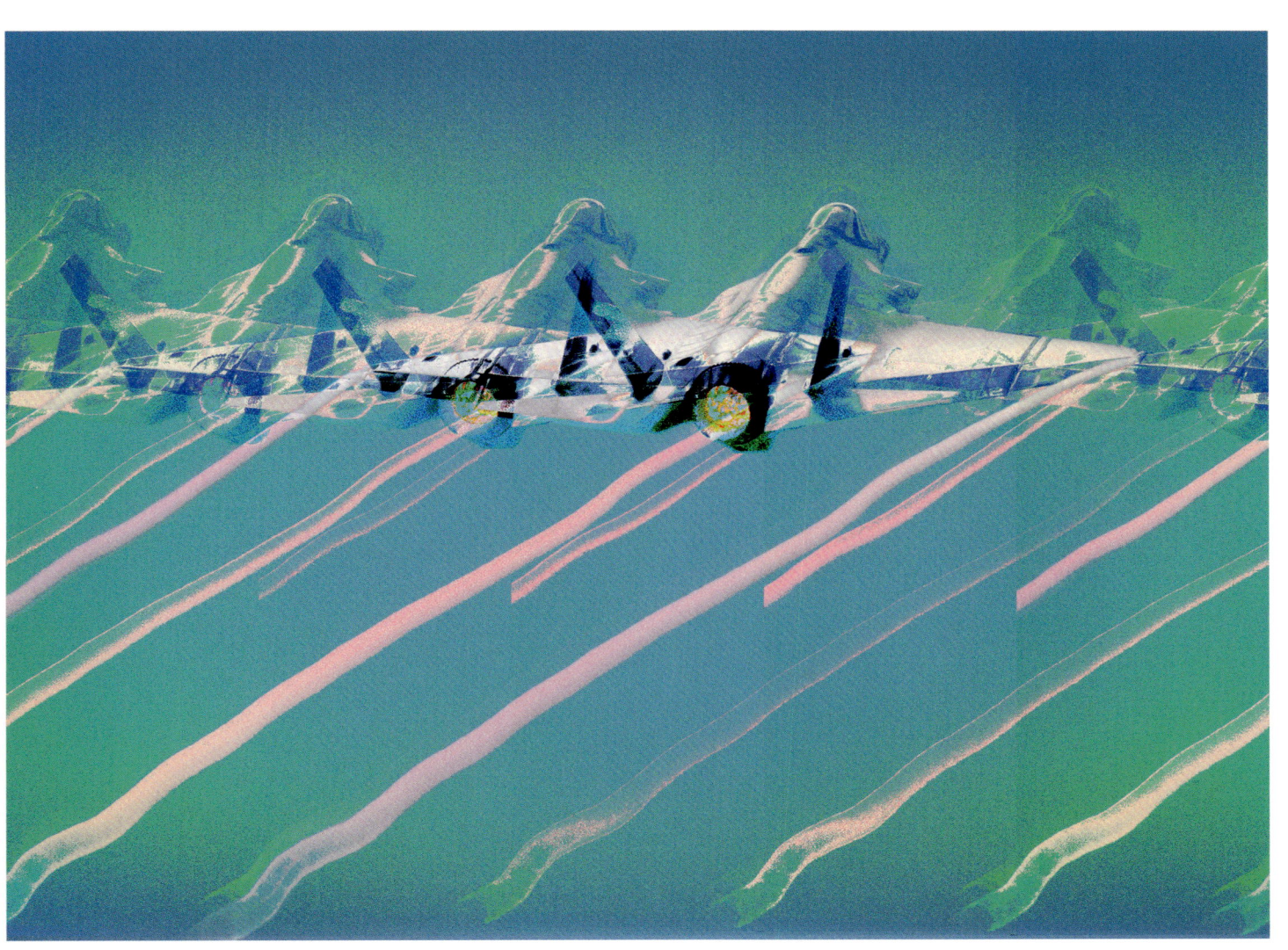

PLATELIST

ACTIONABLE INTELLIGENCE AND CRITICAL SPECULATION:
The Declassified Works of Evan Hume

In ideal flying conditions, a supersonic jet will break the sound barrier flying at just over 767 miles, or 1,234 kilometers, per hour. At this velocity, the metal's friction against the air will generate drag as the two systems, the aircraft and its immediate environment, move in opposite directions. An ear-popping transonic boom will generate a small explosion of excited molecules, and a static cloud will mark the precise moment at which that threshold was reached. Artist Evan Hume takes the idea of this threshold as his subject of study. In one iteration of his photographic research, a jet bursts through this agitated air against a clear blue sky and above a thin layer of cirrus clouds. Unlike its source photograph in the possession of the United States Navy, Hume's two systems above the clouds are the color of a "television tuned to a dead channel."[1]

Hume transforms declassified material that was formerly in the custody of US governmental bodies, such as the Federal Bureau of Investigation, the Central Intelligence Agency, the Department of Defense, and other departments of the military. Despite his donors' sluggishly, begrudgingly bestowed source material and the archives' dispersed information, Hume's photoworks are timely artifacts that slow, even if just for a moment, the flow of intelligence data's mass accretion that has been exponentially accumulating within the past century. Hume committed to this methodology when he began his work on UFOs during his master's program at George Washington University in Washington, DC. The abstract quality of many UFO photographs from those files attracted a certain convergence of abstraction, transmediation, and visual knowledge. Drawn to the UFO photographs' manipulation or complete fabrication, in the hands of certain audiences, abstracted "evidence" would lend itself to broader intercalations of uniquely political conspiracy, especially within the Cold War's military-industrial complex.

As he came into contact with more and more images and documents related to the use of photo-graphic technologies deployed in reconnaissance and surveillance, Hume found that while plenty of photographs were legible, so many more were distorted and so heavily redacted they were rendered unintelligible. While he began to use more of the representational photographs as well as those that had been transformed through reproduction, he identified a tension between the available information related to weapons testing, surveillance, and the indeterminacy of those

---

1 William Gibson, *Neuromancer* (New York: Ace Books, 2000).

sources. As if to fill in the blank spots on the map, as Trevor Paglen describes geographic areas redacted for reasons of national security, Hume adopted the source material's visual idioms to offer new speculative postulations.

"To be sure," Walter Benjamin writes, "only a redeemed mankind receives the fullness of its past— which is to say, only for a redeemed mankind has its past become citable in all its moments."[2] For all of the redaction, the obfuscation, the bureaucratic wild-goose chases and red tape, the past indeed carries with it a temporal and visual index that refers it to redemption, and Hume's photoworks are one step closer to that.

Actionable Intelligence

There is a marked difference between the US Navy's source photograph and Hume's transformed photograph *F/A-18 Hornet* (2020). His, a scanned and digitized photograph, is reduced to the pixels' bits of data, translated into machine-readable 0s and 1s, where the zeroes flip to ones when they reach the necessary electrical threshold. Hume's former photograph is then read as linear data and reduced into bitmap, its smallest components of information. Hume further transforms this once-visual data in audio software, like Adobe Audition or Audacity. However, audio software was not designed to support images, and mistranslated bits of data will yield only "error." Successfully translated bits will output dynamic results, which are legible in the newly transformed images' pixelated striations, RGB arrays of color, or multiplied subjects—digital artifacts from the deliberately imperfect translation process. As Captain George Wheeler of the then-brand-new United States Geological Survey once described of Timothy O'Sullivan's survey photographic practice, these photographs are the necessary reduction of topographical information mapped onto a two-dimensional surface.[3]

The translation of the visual image into audio software and then back into image mirrors the transformation of sound in a supersonic jet and its shock wave. The disconnection between the image and its sound waves emulates a space- and time-based distance between the photograph and its noise. This fabricated Doppler effect attempts to curate an aesthetically perceptive vantage from one visual axis as sound and image are rendered in one transmuted photograph, which shortens the distance between the observer and the event. Archival footage and the use of the authoritative archive itself attempts this closure.

In process and product, the two-dimensional jet's sound and image are pictured simultaneously, incompatible with three-dimensional reality. A similar manipulation of sound and picture, Bruce

---

2   Walter Benjamin, "Theses on the Philosophy of History," in *Illuminations: Essays and Reflections*, ed. Hannah Arendt (New York: Schocken Books, 2016), 254.
3   Robin Kelsey, "Viewing the Archive: Timothy O'Sullivan's Photographs for the Wheeler Survey, 1871–74," *The Art Bulletin* 85, no. 4 (December 2003): 708.

Conner's *Crossroads* (1976), is an antecedent to Hume's work. In the short film, the underwater detonation of the Baker test in mid-1946 is photographed by five hundred cameras at multiple, synchronous angles from circling, unmanned aircraft,[4] temporally layered from different vantages and distances. Like Conner, Hume has altered the audience's aesthetic distance, bringing us closer and closer to the weapon and the terror of its deployment. Like Hume, Conner also requested declassified footage of the test from the National Archives. However, Conner was under strict instructions not to manipulate the film or insert commentary that might endanger national security.[5] In his own way of manipulating the distance between the weapon and his viewers, Conner set the moving image to a dramatic synth score and elongated the time between the blast and its sound wave. Hume's digital recombination of the jet with its attending shock wave thereby manipulates the structural relationship of sound to picture, as its sound waves are mapped incongruously onto its light waves.

Hume reinterprets this challenge in his cyanotype montage *Equivalents* (2020), using the process in which the subject of a photograph is applied directly to light-sensitive material. Hume sought out materials related to the atomic bomb tests at Bikini Atoll, and was able to use the cyan-treated printing process to measure the weapon's luminosity, even from a great and relatively safe distance. Cyanotypes, in color and in process, can indeed provide a qualitative measurement of explosions, which Hume has included from at least eleven vantages from the air to the ground. Mirroring the rectangular shapes of the photographs, strips of beige masking tape make up squares as if to affix them once again to a flat surface, like a bulletin board or a wall. But the surface we try to fixate on recedes further and further away. Hume performs a subtle trompe l'oeil. He scanned each element separately, each cyanotype and strip of masking tape, and arranged them together digitally. The pieces he pieced together—the source material, the transformed material, the flat surface on which they are applied, the information the material claims to offer—resist, as a whole and then individually, the meaning we try to make of these difficult and sometimes incomprehensible images. Instead, like the collage, our fragile and superficial understanding of the systems of representation and access to those systems seems to hang off and float away from our understanding of the picture plane, and their fabricated tempo, the intersecting angles of the cameras' lenses and their arrangement, are only "blinks"[6] of incomprehensible yet somehow actionable intelligence.

Critical Speculation

Another work, *The Million-Dollar Photograph* (2020), is a photographic schema of an immense structure. Thick lines of a structure and xeroxed lines of tape stack against a staticky background,

---

4 Ross Lipman, "Conservation at a Crossroads: Ross Lipman on the Restoration of a Film by Bruce Conner," *Art Forum* (October 2013): 273.

5 Ibid.

6 Howard Eiland and Kevin McLaughlin, "Translators' Forward," in *The Arcades Project*, by Walter Benjamin (Cambridge: Belknap Press, 1999), xi.

striated like a security-lined envelope. Hume separately photographed his studio's corkboard, photographs, and thumbtacks and digitally collaged them together. The layers float on top of one another, almost like an exploded-view illustration. We can see the individual pieces separated, coming into view as an assemblage of materials oriented toward their rightful place in the frame but just slightly off. The thumbtacks' shadows are just visible enough to trick our eye but their exact, multiplied sameness in angle and shading cannot fool us into thinking we have the whole picture.

A figure of a large structure, labeled *The Million-Dollar Photograph* and captioned "Saratov Engels Airfield," outlines the possibility of other structures significant to Soviet operations. *The Million-Dollar Photograph* suggests the connection between the structure and its name. Its monetary description suggests the prerequisite labor that attended the photograph's acquisition. While President Eisenhower expressed mixed feelings about flying in Soviet-restricted airspace, in the service of reconnaissance the necessity outweighed the concerns. To keep tensions cool between the Soviet Union and the United States, Eisenhower offered the use of civilian airfields and aircrafts and even extended an invitation to Nikita Khrushchev to surveil American airfields—a reciprocal, if scurrilous, invitation Khrushchev almost immediately declined.[7] In sensitive times, this was often the presidents' reliable positions, their modus operandi being their consistent oscillation between ambitions for actionable intelligence and aversion to escalation, in this case, from a cold to a heated war.

Below to the left of this document is a picture of two nondescript buildings, one with ten rows of windows exactly the same length and height apart, a bilaterally symmetrical, copy-paste architecture. To that photograph's right is a diagram of a building, titled "National Photographic Interpretation Center," where a photograph points to each floor, one through six. All together— the schema of the "Saratov Engels Airfield," the copy and scanned photograph of the buildings' façade, the diagram of the floors with their attending photographs—the eye attempts to make sense of these pictures as a whole. When faced with incomprehensible information, the eye labors to find patterns and associations. Even further, when positioned as materials on a corkboard, Hume almost postulates some connection between these pieces of information. But their layers of subtle assembly, the composition's artifacts of repeated scanning, and the patina of replication betray the eye. They are a mathematical theorem without the proof.

This is Hume's method of acquiring intelligence: tracking identification numbers, calling the FOIA office, leaving messages, and receiving calls back from a restricted number. Through Freedom of Information Act requests and dogged research into the archives, he seeks out source material from the Federal Bureau of Investigation, the Central Intelligence Agency, and other arms of the US government. To file a request in Washington, DC, a seeker of such clandestine information

7 Gregory W. Pedlow and Donald E. Weizenbach, "U-2 Operations in the Soviet Bloc and Middle East, 1959–1968," in *The Central Intelligence and Overhead Reconnaissance: The U-2 and OXCART Programs, 1954–1974*, 96. IDP Registry no. EO-1998–00299.

must register an account with the FOIA office, submit an identification number, fax the request, and allow fifteen business days for a reply. A seeker should make sure the information is not already freely available, by cross-referencing the request with already declassified documents in the office's database. As can be expected, there are several exemptions: trade secrets and commercial or financial information obtained from outside the government; information from inside a personal residence; and investigation records, especially those relating to domestic violence. Also not allowed: investigatory records compiled for law-enforcement purposes that may interfere with enforcement, council, or ongoing investigations; documents that may disclose the identity of a confidential source or endanger the life of law-enforcement personnel; information specifically authorized by federal law under criteria established by a presidential executive order; and information exempt from at least sixteen articles of the Freedom of Information Act.[8]

With scrupulous attention to the contours of the act, and at times, simply, luck, Hume began requesting documents. His previous attention to the Air Force's Project Blue Book, which involved clandestine research on UFOs from 1947 to 1969, led him to other associations between governmental departments and noteworthy projects conducted during the Cold War. One of these speculative connections was the State Department's Office of International Information and Cultural Affairs' financial involvement with the Museum of Modern Art's exhibition *Advancing American Art*, from 1947.[9] The mission behind the exhibition was to demonstrate to the world that the United States was not solely an aggressive and warring superpower but one that promoted culture and the arts, a reputation it had not yet fulfilled. Even the term "advancing" in the exhibition's title suggested the former reputation's relation with its imperialist agenda in fighting Communism. In 2010, Hume further investigated this connection between the government and its arts initiative and submitted a FOIA request to the CIA for any and all documents related to the CIA's art collection. They granted his request—ten years later—and supplied documents relating to a 1991 exhibition hosted at CIA headquarters in Langley, Virginia, with art from the Melzac art collection. Photographs of the exhibited artworks were redacted.

It could be easy to conflate Hume's redacted pages with readings of pure abstraction. When faced with incomplete or incomprehensible information, Hume has said that that information is abstracted or non-representational, with any facticity the material may have once contained nullified into solid black blocks of redaction. One of Hume's works, *Recon02-50* (2020), transformed through his scanning and manipulation process, is an almost completely censored form. Its provenance is completely unknown and, outside Hume's own procedural breadcrumbs within his internet history, documentation, call logs (and keystrokes stored in a National Security Agency server somewhere in Nevada), completely unknowable. In the context of the other documents

---

8 Code of the District of Columbia, "§ 2–534 Exemptions from disclosure," https://code.dccouncil.us/dc/council/code/sections/2-534.html. Made available through the District of Columbia Law Library.
9 Louis Menand, "Unpopular Front: American Art and the Cold War," *The New Yorker*, October 9, 2005.

Hume takes as his source material, we can trust the work is a converted, official document; first through censoring, then through digital conversion. Only the words "Fighting in the war against terrorism" are legible. To serve as actionable intelligence, it might benefit the public to know in a few bulleted terms what the document names as a potential course of action against terrorism. Instead the reader is left with a blacked-out, hash-shaded, informationally arid plane, and the only visual information outside of these blocks of non-information are lines that could suggest it was some kind of form in the first place. Its status as intelligence confounds its supply of intelligence, and when rendered as an art form, it is a picture that certainly resists being a picture.

The paradox of these documents is that they are declassified after decades of obfuscation, and the shreds of information that are not redacted offer little to no visual or literal information. So many photographs and material documents donated, in a sense, by the FBI, the CIA, and the US Air Force lack the intelligence for which they were withheld from the public. At another time, Hume received pieces of microfilm in one of his requests, and again, they were so heavily redacted that they too offered little to no information. While abstracted intelligence/intelligent abstraction offers at least some texture of visual material in its scanned artifacts, like striation marks on processed film, Hume's redacted source material absorbs speculation without reflecting any information back. Pushing aside for a moment the textured blackness of Hume's association with modernist abstraction, in Hume's censored works, the redaction shares physical and conceptual features with the trademarked color Vantablack. Vantablack's physical capacity to absorb 99.965% of all visible light on the electromagnetic spectrum allows such little and negligible refraction of visible information, it simulates Hume's redacted pages. In a figurative sense, Kazimir Malevich's black squares are also a fitting connection to make, as they are visual metaphors for the absence of information but ones that can offer something back in exchange for our critical speculation.

Formulated by Nikolai Fedorovich Fedorov and published in 1906, *filosofiia obshchego dela* (the philosophy of the common task) is the Russian Cosmist and Christian dictum that to emulate Christ, one must believe in the resurrection as well as the humanistic and technological resurrection of the dead. After death, the deceased are never wholly deceased; one's atoms are collected and reconstituted. Ideologically dependent on the law of conservation of mass—that matter is neither created nor destroyed—reconstitution has faith in the classical maxim "nothing comes from nothing," a supranatural conviction of atomic nature.[10] It is an expression of faith in the fabric of the spiritual world and what it can offer the physical. Like Paul Klee's *Angelus Novus*, the angel of history "would like to stay, awaken the dead, and make whole what has been smashed."[11] In that way, it might be in the absence of information that the atomic, the physical, the informative are illuminated.

---

10 Asif A. Siddiq, "Imagining the Cosmos: Utopians, Mystics, and the Popular Culture of Spaceflight in Revolutionary Russia," *Osiris* 23, no. 1 (2008): 267–68.
11 Walter Benjamin, "Theses on the Philosophy of History," in *Illuminations: Essays and Reflections*, ed. Hannah Arendt (New York: Schocken Books, 2007), 257.

In another work, *Commentary on the Art of Photography* (2020), Hume positions an excerpt of a text against an unseen flat surface, its only suggestion of that surface being the masking tape surrounding the 8½" x 11" document. In Hume's signature mode, the document and its support show signs of scanning and reprinting. The document's text suggests that it is a continuation of a longer document. In medias res, the end of a sentence is the beginning of the composition and the original text subtly cut off by the margins supported by the original printer's setting. Two blocks of blackout, one hand-cut and the other hand-torn presumably stacked in one of the copying processes, absorb the bottom third of the composition. "After all, what is a photographer?," one of the passages reads, "Someone who makes photographs not with a retoucher's brush and a knife, but with a camera." This is an informative scrap that aptly caught Hume's attention in the thousands of documents he has pored over in his career. Having snatched the document from the flow of data, Hume exhibits the work, almost as a distortedly textual yet ever-photographic self-portrait. For some of his photoworks, Hume often uses a handheld scanner and Photoshop, the digital tools of his photographic trade. In the beginning, his practice involved little distortion and manipulation, which mimicked the materials' rigidity and, by extension, the procedure by which Hume acquired them. The source of this document is unknown, but that Hume found this document, in its abridged or perhaps its whole form, is a curious case of a redacted document that was formerly in the government's custody. Nevertheless, this is an abbreviated treatise on the role of the photographer that Hume has methodically framed according to the modus operandi of the original documents' contemporaries: mounted on a bulletin board on an unknown floor in a nondescript building, and on display for Washington bureaucrats who were fighting in the Cold War.

"He makes his decisions according to what he knows," another passage reads, and "in judging his decision we are judging his whole experience." Keeping with Hume's criticality, we might exchange *judging* with *speculating*. It is unlikely that the intention of the document's author was for a single page of his treatise to make it into government custody, and even less a photowork. Therefore, this piece's place in the body of work that is an artist's monograph, and further removed from another body of work—the assemblage of custodial, governmental bodies—offers a new context through which we can critically speculate its meaning and purpose. "If the subject is small in scale," the document continues, "understanding may be derived at first hand." However, Hume's translation and mutation across mediums complicates this seemingly simple assertion.

When used in the service of war, even a cold one, the photograph is a product of weapons testing, technological development, and surveillance. During the Manhattan Project's Trinity Test, the Optics Division leaders Julian Mack and Berlyn Brixner organized thousands of photographs of the detonation of the first atomic bomb, later to be compiled and translated into graphs that measured the radius, heat, blisters, spikes, and time of ground strike. Each camera was operated by an explosive detonator, a trigger, and the mirrors rotated using a turbine, which according to

Brixner was not entirely reliable.[12] Though, by most accounts, the camera worked as it should. However, Brixner said that the optics and spectroscopics engineer Morris Patapoff "didn't like the pictures we were getting and said we were getting just optical illusions really, photographing optical illusions."[13] The photographs from the camera showed that the implosion process of the mock atomic bombs were not what Patapoff "thought the implosion process should be doing."[14] When Brixner's team developed the camera further, their photo experiments demonstrated that it was the implosion process itself, not the photographic technology, that was at fault. Optical illusions, or if we can speculate further, "mechanical abstractions," in fact represented a reality outside prediction.

Mechanical abstraction—the only actionable intelligence available to the public—and the speculation it commands is form and method to Hume's work. From his layered and hovering compositions to his color transformations to his methodical transmutation of photographs, Hume's photoworks demonstrate the process of his photographic practice as abstracted, actionable intelligence and critical speculation. He shifts our attention to the structures that surveil us, defend us, make information available to us. His photoworks are political exercises whereby the photograph, or whatever form the work takes, is the byproduct. The works themselves are not evidence of clandestine operations. They are evidence of the very procedure by which we can inherit knowledge of those operations.

E.N. da C. Andrade, a physics historian writing on cloud chamber images in the 1920s, writes, "Whatever may be the fate of the theories which have been so inadequately exposed in this book, whatever modifications of mishaps they may meet, the experimental facts which led to their formation, and those others to whose discovery they in their turn give rise, will remain as definite knowledge to form a lasting ornament to an age otherwise rich in manifold disaster and variety of evil change." These are the quandaries that confound, and support, Hume's photoworks. "Systems are hard to photograph," Rebecca Solnit writes, "but consequences are not."[15] Hume's task is to bring together a body of work that attempts to do both.

—Lily Brewer

---

12 Berlyn Brixner, "A High-Speed Rotating-Mirror Frame Camera," *Journal of the SMPTE* 59 (December 1952): 503–11.
13 Berlyn Brixner, "Berlyn Brixner's Interview," interview by Yvonne Delamater, *Voices of the Manhattan Project*, February 22, 1992, https://www.manhattanprojectvoices.org/oral-histories/berlyn-brixners-interview.
14 Ibid.
15 Rebecca Solnit, "The Visibility Wars," in *Invisible: Covert Operations and Classified Landscapes*, by Trevor Paglen (New York: Aperture, 2010), 10.

ACKNOWLEDGMENTS

I am beyond grateful for the encouragement, generosity, and support of my work that made this book possible. I would especially like to thank:

Malena Magnolia

Glenn & Julie Hume

Bob & Carol Hume

Christine Devine

Frank Devine

Adam Leighton & Kanako Kashima

Dean Kessmann

Troy Aiken

James Alefantis

Todd Crocken

Mike Rippy